Elvis Don't Like Football

Elvis
DON'T LIKE
FOOTBALL

The Life and Raucous Times of the NFL's Most Outspoken Coach

Jerry Glanville

and J. David Miller

Macmillan Publishing Company • New York

Collier Macmillan Canada • Toronto

Maxwell Macmillan International

New York • Oxford • Singapore • Sydney

Macmillan Publishing Company
866 Third Avenue, New York, NY 10022
Collier Macmillan Canada, Inc.
1200 Eglinton Avenue East, Suite 200
Don Mills, Ontario M3C 3N1

Permission notices for song lyrics quoted in this book appear on page 191.

Library of Congress Cataloging-in-Publication Data
Glanville, Jerry.
    Elvis don't like football : the life and raucous times of the
NFL's most outspoken coach / Jerry Glanville with J. David Miller.
        p.   cm.
    ISBN 0-02-544011-X
    1. Glanville, Jerry.   2. Football—United States—Coaches—
Biography.   I. Miller, J. David (Joseph David), 1964–
II. Title.
GV939.G54A3   1990   90-33745   CIP
796.332′092—dc20
[B]

Design by Paolo Pepe

Macmillan books are available at special discounts for bulk purchases for sales promotions, premiums, fund-raising, or educational use. For details, contact:

Special Sales Director
Macmillan Publishing Company
866 Third Avenue
New York, NY 10022

10 9 8 7 6 5 4 3 2 1

Printed in the United States of America

This book is dedicated to Jerry Jeff Walker, Kris Kristofferson and John Cougar Mellencamp, the last true rebels of our time . . .
—Jerry Glanville

This book is dedicated to my mother, Jayne Gagliardi, who never quite understood me but loved me anyway . . .
—J. David Miller

Contents

Acknowledgments   ix
1: Elvis Is in the Kitchen   1
2: Life Without Football Is Not Life   9
3: Living on the Edge   25
4: The Man in Black   42
5: Hit the Beach   57
6: Two Tickets to Paradise   65
7: A Wrestler, The President and a Dead Guy   74
8: My Hero, Chuck Noll   85
9: Motorcycles, Rabbits and Jerry Jeff   97
10: "I Feel Like Hank Williams Tonight"   108
11: Snakebites, Gator Bait and a Dog
    Named Rusty   118
12: If You Don't Like Me, I Probably Didn't
    Like You First   130
13: Livin' Close to the Bone   140
14: "Taking Every Wrong Direction on My
    Lonely Way Back Home"   157
Epilogue   178
Index   183

Acknowledgments

There is no way to express proper thanks to my mother, Helen, who taught me the two most important lessons of my life: Never give up and be totally color-blind.

Equally important is the love of my wife, Brenda, and son, Justin; their faith and courage make life an overwhelming victory.

To my brother, Richard, I offer this line from Kris Kristofferson's "The Eagle and the Bear": "I will help my brother and we'll sink or swim together, and if you don't like it, mister, I don't care."

My best to (Houston-based) KPRC talk-show host Anita Martini, who stands tall in the face of criticism and prefers truth and honesty over sensational headlines.

And finally, my prayers to Father Jim Alcorn at Texas Children's Hospital. The chance to share my life with hundreds of children was a heart-changing experience and taught me to appreciate the precious value of life itself.

—Jerry Glanville

The unlikely team of unsung heroes who helped in the two-year production of *Elvis* was led by June Jones, who believed in this project when others doubted. My thanks also to Darrel "Mouse" Davis, who will someday receive the credit owed to him by his peers. A pat on the back goes to Steve Watterson, a treasured friend who answered all my pleas for help. And regards to my many associates who helped along the way.

Special thanks to my agent, Brian Zevnik, whose loyalty and dedication to the cause made great things happen. Kudos also to Macmillan's Rick Wolff, who displayed remarkable patience, understanding and ability for an Ivy League editor.

Finally, my thanks to Roy Exum and all the other insecure people in my life who attempted unsuccessfully to harness my drive and desire. Kicking me from the snug security of the nest taught me to fly, thereby pushing me to heights I never dreamed possible.

—J. David Miller

I've got to wonder
What my daddy would've done
If he'd seen the way they turned this dream around
I've got to go by what he told me
Try to tell the truth
And stand my ground
Don't let the bastards get you down.

—Kris Kristofferson
"Third World Warrior"

Elvis Don't Like Football

1

Elvis Is in the Kitchen

I started believing that Elvis Presley wasn't really dead during training camp before the 1988 season. My quarterback coach at the time, June Jones, had heard some woman on a radio talk show arguing that Elvis was still alive. We had a lot of laughs about that until somebody sent *us* a tape of a recent telephone conversation with Elvis. I swear, it was him.

That preseason we were playing New England in Memphis, Tennessee, home of the King. June was riding to practice with me when I decided that on Saturday I would leave tickets for Elvis at the will-call window, and maybe, just maybe, the King would show up at the game. June laughed when I told him what I had in mind.

"In fact, I heard that Elvis just appeared again on a California radio station," June said.

"Do you think he can make it back for the game?" I asked.

That's how the idea started.

That afternoon we told the local press that Elvis would

have two tickets at will call. My phone started ringing off the hook—people were spotting Elvis everywhere, Elvis was calling local radio stations, Elvis was eating chicken in the park, Elvis was a doorman at the Peabody, Elvis was leaving messages at my hotel.

The next day, I offered him a job. I told the media that we didn't care how fat Elvis was, he was welcome on our ball club. Besides, Steve Watterson, our strength coach, could knock pounds off John Candy. Steve could've had Elvis bench-pressing 350 pounds in a matter of weeks. But even if Elvis didn't lose any weight, we could've found something for him to do. I never really did understand why Elvis was so concerned about his weight. A lot of my favorite people, like Buddy Ryan, are overweight. Elvis shouldn't have to take that crap.

When we finally came out to play New England in the Liberty Bowl, there were huge photos of Elvis draped everywhere. In the east end zone was a huge sign: "Jerry, I'm Here—Elvis." Most people thought some crazy fan had hung that sign up, but I've got a secret to tell you: Elvis really *was* in the stadium that day. In fact, I got him in the game at tight end, and I've got the official play-by-play sheet to prove it. Late in the game, our backup quarterback, Cody Carlson, faded back and threw a 16-yard pass down the middle to Elvis. He dropped it, but I thought it was a heckuva effort for a fifty-four-year-old fat guy who hadn't made a public appearance in eleven years. The NFL play-by-play sheet reads: "Carlson pass incomplete, intended for Elvis Presley." Looking back on that, Elvis probably would've played better at offensive tackle, as big as he was. But I told him that in his heyday, he should have been a running back. After all, he really had some moves; he was a swivel-hipped guy.

Houston fans eventually learned to keep one eye on the field and the other on our sideline, because you never knew what we were up to. On that particular day, we had Elvis surrounded by a bunch of rookies and free agents—I'm sure most people thought he was just another overweight, out-of-shape guy. And trust me, that year, we had a lot of first-year guys who looked like that. We had one kid, an offensive tackle, who came in at 350 pounds. He looked like someone sat in his lap and didn't leave. If Elvis was standing next to him, it's no wonder the fans didn't see him. The media missed him, too, but it's because they were looking the wrong way. Kenny Hand, a reporter for the *Houston Post*, sat outside the will-call window for the entire time, waiting for Elvis to show up. He was miffed afterward, because he missed the whole game. He was even more upset when he saw the play-by-play sheet!

Elvis disappeared immediately after the game—he didn't turn in his uniform, or shower, which honestly surprised me. When I got back to Houston, I was greeted by a crush of Elvis mail and gifts. A man in England called my office to say that he'd seen Elvis making cole-slaw at a Kentucky Fried Chicken. Fans sent me Elvis's will, driver's license and license plate. Joe Theismann sent me his favorite Elvis photo, complete with the King's autograph. Another fan sent me a picture of him wearing a football helmet. My general manager at the time, Ladd Herzeg, gave me a collector's liquor decanter of Elvis that plays "Kentucky Rain."

Then there was this letter from promoter Larry McBride, the guy who discovered the country band Alabama and now runs "Glowbal" Records, Inc.:

> Dear Coach:
> Please accept this letter as your invitation to join us in the Glowbal search for the King. I realize you have a tough, demanding schedule, but you might find this a pleasant stress break. It will be fun. Give me a call!

McBride told me he planned to "comb the globe" in search of Elvis, and he wanted me to ride around with him. "We'll stop at nothing, spare no expense," he said. The *London Sun* said it would part with $1.75 million if anyone could bring Elvis in alive. Now *that* got my attention. You'd have to coach a lot of football to make $1.75 million, so I made up my mind; the next time I saw Elvis, I'd get him to come out in public and we'd split the cash.

After the New England game, we'd been back in Houston about four weeks when Hurricane Gilbert threatened to smash the Texas coast, so we were forced to look elsewhere for a place to practice. Memphis had been great to us, so we packed up the team and moved practice to Tennessee for a few days before our game in New York against the Jets. After our first day of practice in Memphis, we loaded up a whole bus full of players and coaches and headed to Graceland, hoping to convince Elvis to go back with us to Houston.

Graceland was amazing. More people visit Graceland each year than the White House. In 1988, the year we dropped by, 640,000 people paid $7 for the tour. The value of Elvis's estate has grown to more than $50 million, from only $4.9 million on the day he allegedly died at the age of forty-two in 1977. Our tour guide told us that if the present trend continues, by the year 2000 one out of every twelve people in America will be an Elvis impersonator.

A couple of things fascinated me right away. At one point in his life, Elvis Presley must have loved the National Football League, because Graceland is full of television sets. In one room alone, he had five TVs on one wall! When I saw that, I assumed that Elvis kept an eye on every game he could tune in at one time.

We had been through the entire house—without a trace of the Big E—when something else caught our attention. Doug Shively, our defensive line coach, smelled peanut butter outside the kitchen and asked our tour guide if we could investigate. The guide insistently said no and blocked the door leading to the kitchen. That's when we heard silverware clinking around and some other very suspicious noises. And the peanut butter smell kept getting stronger, which convinced me Elvis was busy mixing up one of his 3,000-calorie fried peanut-butter-and-banana sandwiches.

Elvis *was* in the kitchen. If Shive had been a few years younger, he might have body-blocked the guide and charged the kitchen. Everybody knows Elvis loves to eat, but it broke my heart that he would rather eat than hang around with some good ol' boys who had come all the way from Houston to see him. The fastest way to Elvis's heart is through his stomach.

Subsequently, though, in the past year, I've given a lot of thought to Elvis. Next to James Dean, another one of my heroes, Elvis is my favorite. And I find it too easy to believe he *is* alive. Remember, this is a guy who got special permission to dig up his brother and rebury him at Graceland. And after his mother was buried there, he specifically said he wanted to be buried next to her. Then, after all that trouble, his own daddy supposedly misspells Elvis's middle name—Aaron, instead of Aron—on his tombstone and buries him next to his grandfather.

Then there's his life insurance policy. It is illegal to collect on a life insurance policy if that person isn't really dead. Elvis has a million-dollar policy that has never been collected. Why?

I get mail from people every day with convincing evidence. Gail Brewer-Georgio, who has authored a best-seller on Elvis told me that "there is enough evidence to raise serious questions about whether he ever died."

Here's a good question: If he's dead, why does he keep coming to see us play? He's been spotted at more than a dozen Houston home games in the last two years; I've personally seen him twice, wearing a black leather jacket and sunglasses. And I get letters every month from Elvis, congratulating me on victories, complimenting my outfits.

All the letters, by the way, are postmarked Pasadena, Texas.

I respect Elvis. He was the first guy to really be an entertainer, to live on the edge, to make people happy. I can really relate to some of his songs, like "In the Ghetto," "The Trilogy," and, especially, "Kentucky Rain." I lived in the South for twenty-seven years, which explains why I like "The Trilogy." And when I first started coaching, I lived with Joe Bugel, who is now the head coach of the Phoenix Cardinals, in a log cabin in Kentucky. It had only one bed, so we flipped for it and I lost. Whenever it rained, water dripped on the floor where I slept, thus my affection for "Kentucky Rain." The closest I ever came to the ghetto was growing up in Detroit. If you grew up in the fifties, when Elvis was the hottest thing alive, you remember him as a guy who attracted all age groups. And he still does. Elvis was probably the first guy that was loved by not only teenagers, but also parents. It's amazing how many people still love Elvis. On airplanes, in cabs, in hotels, people walk up to me and talk about Elvis. Once we were on an airplane and a stewardess came by and gave me three Elvis albums—it happens all the time.

His music will never die. In 1988, the Presley estate earned $15 million as a direct result of tourism and licensing of Elvis products, and to date, Elvis has earned more gold records than *any* recording star. It amazes me that my eight-year-old son, Justin, sings the same Elvis songs that people who are seventy years old still listen to. That's what I call a broad audience.

The other day I was opening my mail and found a poster-size blowup of an incredible photograph, taken four months after the supposed death of Elvis by a Chicago businessman touring Graceland. It was verified by Kodak, after careful examination, as having been processed correctly, and Kodak also confirmed that it had not been altered in any way. In the photo, taken next to Graceland, is a small, one-story home, and Elvis is looking out through a screen door. I'm sure Elvis, watching the parade of well-wishers go by outside, was touched by the public's show of affection.

I'll always wonder, though, how Elvis could walk away from the Houston Oilers. Maybe he was embarrassed about dropping that pass. maybe he just decided he don't like football. Singers and football players are a lot alike— you wear tight pants and jump around a lot, but then again, nobody ever blindsided a singer. I still say Elvis should've coached in the AFC Central against guys like Chuck Noll and Sam Wyche. Now that's a reason to fake your own death.

But Elvis is welcome on my team any time. And if you see him, tell him the Atlanta Falcons are the new kings of rock and roll.

2

Life Without Football Is Not Life

When I was growing up, we lived in a $16-a-month federal housing project on Detroit's East Side. As a kid, everything in my life was based on cars. My daddy sold cars, and if he had a good month, I got a new baseball mitt. If he wasn't selling any cars, then the whole family sucked it up until he sold a few. He sold Fords, then Mercurys. I remember he always had a brand-new demo, the fastest new Ford they were making. It was great. There was nothing more fun than screaming around in my dad's latest, hottest Mercury. That started my love for fast, old cars.

I had my own paper route, on the East Side, when I was thirteen years old. You were supposed to be sixteen to have a paper route, but I had lied about my age and bought my own route. You had to buy a route; nobody gave you one. But my father really believed that there was never anything that came free that was worth having anyway. So I worked my paper route, seven days a week. Once, on one of those mysterious, dark and stormy nights like you read about in detective novels, a guy approached me. He smarted off to me, and I laughed at him. He pulled out a gun and robbed me, then shot me in the eye. It was a BB gun, and the BB lodged down in the lower part of my eye.

They took me to Saratoga Hospital for treatment. I was the only guy in the hospital with a gunshot wound. Everybody else had knife wounds. Today in Detroit, it's the other way around. The number one cause of death among youths in Detroit today is lead poisoning. But they operated on me right then and there and saved my eye. Meanwhile, my older brother, Richard, and my dad went back and waited on the guy. They found him.

"You made out a lot better than he did," Richard told me later, smiling.

That's just the way we lived during those times. As a kid, violence was just a part of life. I fought in school every single day. Sometimes, when it got real bad, I'd run home to change, because I'd get a whipping if I tore up my good clothes. So I'd put my Levi's on and go out and fight like a man.

It seemed like every day something violent happened. My best friend and I were playing baseball together on the playground when somebody accidentally hit him over the head with the bat. It killed him. Nothing sticks in your mind more than being a pallbearer when you're in the sixth grade. To this day that lives with me. It was like, "Why him? How could this possibly happen?" I hated school, and that made me like it even less, which is evident from my attendance records.

Somebody told me I still hold the record in the Detroit public school system for absenteeism. I will admit—I was one of the best hooky players in history. Anytime the Tigers played at home, my brother and me missed school. One day the school called my father down and they compared the Tigers' home schedule with my absenteeism records. They were identical.

I got into the ball games in various ways. Sometimes I spent my lunch money, sometimes I spent my newspaper money. But getting in without a ticket was my specialty. We climbed over fences, under fences—you name it, we did it. And we watched a lot of baseball without tickets. Maybe that's why I'm so fascinated now with *giving away* tickets.

One time, when I was only eleven, I hopped a streetcar down to Tiger Stadium to see the Tigers play a 5 P.M. game. The only problem was I forget to tell anybody. My mom was sick with worry when I didn't come home from school. She knew I was too ornery and too ugly to be kidnapped, so she figured I had probably been beaten up and left for dead in an alley somewhere. When I finally got home, I didn't see what all the fuss was about.

"I just went to a game," I argued. "What's the deal?"

"*You're eleven years old!*" my mom roared.

Even at that age, I just looked at things a little differently than everybody else. And I continued my treks to Tiger Stadium. In fact, I even watched the 1957 NFL championship, between Cleveland and Detroit, without buying a ticket.

School just didn't appeal to me. It came too easy. I

didn't like being indoors. While my teachers talked and gave out assignments, I'd be looking out the window. Shortly after they dropped the bomb on Hiroshima and Nagasaki, the school gave us blood tests and made us wear dog tags with our blood type. I guess they figured if the bombs fell and somebody got an arm or leg blown off, they'd know what type blood you needed. Now that's motivational.

Detroit then was the industrial capital of the United States, and we assumed if Japan struck back, they'd hit Detroit. So as a kid, we had to put up with constant fake air raids. They were like bad fire drills. You had to run downstairs to the boiler room, where everybody had a spot with their number on it, and you stood on your number. It was a waste of time. I always felt that if all these horrible things were going to happen, if somebody was really going to drop bombs on us, then what the hell, let's go outside and play some ball while we've got a chance. Why be in here, crouching and scared, if somebody's about to blow us away?

As a kid, football was not my sport of choice. I was more interested in baseball. I played doubleheaders every day. I played in every league that would take me. Sometimes my afternoon papers were six hours late because I would go play two games. There were people who waited until eleven o'clock at night just to read their newspaper. But at the time, I never played football. Sometimes my dad would take me to Michigan State games on Saturday, and occasionally my uncle would take me to see the Lions on Sunday. But when I lived in Detroit, I never played a down of football.

When I was fourteen, we moved with our mother to the small bedroom community of Perrysburg, Ohio, just 10 miles south of Toledo. My parents had split up, and my mom went to work at Lion's Department Store in nearby Maumee. My brother always said that if we had stayed in Detroit, both of us would have ended up as residents of the state's penal system. Let's just say it was a critical move.

In eighth grade, I went out for football for the first time. That's when I discovered that I could knock someone down and not get in trouble for it. In those days, I was a 135-pound fullback and linebacker. I couldn't believe it. When I lived in Detroit, if you got in a fight in school, they would take you down to the Police Athletic League gym and make you punch it out with gloves on. Now, all of a sudden, I'm knocking the devil out of people and everybody's saying, "Great job, Jerry, great job." I loved it immediately.

When I was a freshman at Perrysburg High School, they let me play on the freshman team, the junior varsity team and the varsity team. We played the freshman game on Monday, the J.V. game on Thursday and the varsity game on Friday. I was getting a lot of football. Today you're only allowed eight quarters a week. I walked funny all the time, but nobody told me I shouldn't be playing three games a week.

The weirdest thing about my freshman year was I did

an English paper entitled "What I Want To Do With My Life." I wrote that, someday, I'd be the head coach of the Detroit Lions. To this day, people who were in school with me still stop my brother on the street and ask him if I really had my life plotted out, even then. Our head coach, Dave Martin, drove a '55 Ford convertible, the nicest car in town. And he dressed real sharp. Peg pants, the whole bit. Who knows—maybe subconsciously I was already thinking that coaching might not be too bad a lifestyle.

John Whitacre, my English teacher, didn't care for my classroom antics but seemed to sense that I'd somehow do something funny with my life.

"Jerry," he once told me, "I expect to see you on the stage someday in Las Vegas, working as a bad comedian."

By my senior year, I was up to about 215 pounds and had a 19-inch neck. I looked like a fireplug with hair and would hit anything that moved. I had a philosophy: If that's my man, I'm going to rip his head off. In fact, Bob Steinecker, one of the assistant coaches, described me as "just a thug . . . a kid who loves physical contact." The coaches loved my attitude. I was crazy.

I rode a Harley-Davidson to school and to football practice. It was a big old greasy hog and broke down about every other day. My brother, Richard, rode a English-made Triumph, identical to James Dean's bike. We would ride together, dodge traffic together. We were crazy. Once he hit the pavement doing about 75 miles per hour, flew over the median and slid down the road.

Somehow, he managed to cover his face with his arm. When it was over, he had skin on his face and that was about it. They rushed him to the hospital in Bowling Green and wrapped him in gauze and ointment. They told him it would be weeks before he could get out. But at the time, we were also running homemade dragsters at the drag strip, and Richard was our driver. I snuck into the hospital to see him.

"Richard," I said, "you've gotta drive Sunday."

"I can take the pain, Jerry," he said. "But can you get me outta here?"

He was as crazy as me. We carried him out of the hospital, all bundled up in gauze, drove him down to the drag strip and stuffed him in the cockpit of a dragster. He won the race, and we took him back to the hospital. He was a little dirtier when we took him back than he was when we got him.

But I loved motorcycles for one reason: Speed. Nowhere else, except in drag racing, can you get that rush of acceleration. Richard and I would wind out from zero to 100 miles per hour as fast as we could—that's called a "hiccup." What a breathless feeling. It's also when you hit the pavement. I had one bad wreck, but I was more fortunate than my brother. I was roaring through downtown Perrysburg on my way to football practice one afternoon, when some little old lady opened the door of her Ford Falcon right in front of me. There was a tremendous crash, and the next thing I knew, I was sliding down the street on her car door, sparks flying, about 50 miles per hour. I tore the door right off the car! You should have seen the looks people gave me as I slid by them, screaming.

I played football the same way I rode motorcycles. One of my teammates was Roger Miracle, who today works for the Secret Service. He protects President Bush, among others. But back then, he couldn't protect anybody. I'd hit him so hard his helmet would crack. Every single day, I nailed that guy. A few small colleges were looking at me as a linebacker. We went undefeated, 9–0, and won the Great Northern League title, which is more a tribute to our coaches than our players. Our coach, Jack Donaldson, went on to become an assistant coach with the New York Jets, the Cincinnati Bengals and the Buffalo Bills. I learned a lot of football from him, enough to be named Most Valuable Player my senior year.

My heroes back then were guys like Bobby Layne and Doak Walker of the Detroit Lions. On Sundays I'd drive back to Detroit and watch them play at Briggs Stadium. Even back then, I'd chart the schemes they were running, chart the defenses as if we were going to play them. I didn't have a ticket to the 1957 championship game between the Lions and the Browns, but just like old times, I snuck in anyway. The Lions beat them, 59–14, and I still have a spiral notebook where I charted the whole game.

By then, I didn't care too much for baseball, but I played anyway, at Perrysburg. I've always considered baseball boring. Two guys playing catch and seven other guys standing around scratching themselves. But one of my teammates was Jim Leyland, who is now the

Pittsburgh Pirates' manager, and he livened things up a bit. Leyland was crazy, too. We would skip school and go to games. One time the principal caught us skipping school and dragged us back to his office.

"You two guys will never be successful," he yelled at us. "You're always out there playing baseball and football. Neither one of you will end up worth a darn."

A number of schools invited me to visit, so I obliged. When I visited the University of Idaho, I got sidetracked by the rodeo that was in town. I'd always been fascinated by the rodeo. When we lived in Detroit, Richard and I had visited a friend in the country, and my brother thought he was tough enough to ride this wild steer. He came off that steer faster than a hiccup. He was in the eighth grade, I was in the sixth. When he made a face-first dismount, I decided the rodeo wasn't for me. I wasn't that crazy. In Idaho, I saw one helluva rodeo. Those were some real cowboys. I had so much fun I forgot about the school. I never even saw the stadium.

Montana State offered me a good scholarship, and I took it. At Montana, I worked the chutes at the annual college rodeo. I'll never forget the hot, angry breath of those broncs. My job was to swing open Gate 3, and believe me, I got the heck out of the way. Even today, I wonder at the courage and the size of those guys, as compared to the size of the creatures they climb aboard. Especially the bull riders.

Everybody in Montana was a cowboy. They were all the same size. If somebody lost their luggage, it didn't matter; they could all wear each other's clothes. That's when I learned to appreciate nice boots. Leather boots. Only drugstore cowboys wear snake and lizard boots. If you don't believe me, try wearing a pair of snakeskin boots down to Gate 3 in Bozeman, Montana, and see what happens. To this day, I won't wear cheap boots. All my boots are handmade by David Wheeler of Wheeler Boots in Houston, Texas. David wouldn't be caught dead in a pair of snakeskin boots.

Montana turned out to be just too far from home. So I dropped out and went back to Detroit. I ended up on a Chevrolet assembly line, working twelve-hour days and making $110 a week. Just when I thought I would be stuck on an assembly line forever, I received a phone call from Rollie Dotsch, assistant coach at Northern Michigan. He offered me a scholarship, which I gladly accepted.

Believe me—the *only* reason I was there was to play football. Period. My mother wanted me to be an attorney. She bought me about twenty-five legal books, which I still have stashed away somewhere. I've never opened one of them. If being a lawyer was anything like "L.A. Law," then it would be terrific, but most lawyers sit around reading documents, poring over interpretations. Few lawyers ever see a courtroom. But I didn't have what it took to be a doctor or lawyer. You have to love to study and love books to do those kinds of jobs. I hated to study anything but football.

Being a football player, I took the, uh, *easier* courses. I was fortunate enough that I could pass without studying. If I needed to get a B, then I could get a B without much work. If I didn't need a B, then I'd take a C or D. I was good at two things: I could remember anything that was said in class, and I was great at giving impromptu speeches. All my teammates used to make fun of me because in four or five years of college, I never bought any books.

People see "psychology" on my résumé now and assume that I *wanted* to be a psych major. That's not true. The truth is, if you're in college long enough, you will stumble around until you find something you like. I attended a lot of classes, but I hated most of them. I took sociology, and that was more boring than Chuck Noll. I took history, but the teacher was so bad that he ruined it. So I ended up hating history, too, which is odd, because today, I read anything about history I can get my hands on. But then they made me take a general psychology class, and it was interesting, so I took another one. And another one.

Poof. I became a psychology major. I enjoyed mental games, mental chess matches with people. I enjoyed knowing what made people tick. The psychology instructor was a woman named Dr. Rutherford, and she was full of enthusiasm and knew how to motivate you. It wasn't so much the course or the curriculum, it was more like, "I can deal with this, this lady's funny." So from that point on, I took every course she ever taught. Pretty soon I was taking her graduate courses while I was still an undergraduate.

Finally, I called my mother one day and hit her with the bad news.

"Mom," I said, "I'm not going to be a lawyer, or a doctor. I just don't have it."

"Okay, son," she sighed. "But for God's sake, don't go into something stupid."

"Like what?" I asked.

"You know, something stupid, like coaching."

Oh boy. If they could, some NFL fans would probably tell my mother not to worry, that I'm still not a coach.

Occasionally I'd go home to visit, and sometimes my brother, who was in the Navy, would be on leave at the same time. There was a family down the street that had eighteen kids, and my mom took in one of them because their house was too crowded. So when Richard and I were home together, there weren't enough beds. The last guy home at night had to sleep on the sofa. It was usually Richard. But once, late at night, we ran into each other walking home. For four blocks, we got into a very vocal discussion over who would get the bed. It turned into a big fight, right in the middle of the night. Somebody called the police, and the next thing I knew, I was hand-cuffed to a parking meter.

The biggest lesson I learned in college didn't come in a classroom. In fact, my mom will be shocked when she reads this. But it's legend now at Northern Michigan. By the end of my sophomore year, I was just starting to emerge as a football player, and I thrived on violence. I loved to fight. I never backed down from anybody. I developed a running feud with an older guy, an ex-Marine who had been in the Golden Gloves. He popped off, and I popped off, and finally we'd had enough of each other.

I decided I was going to kick his butt. The whole school placed bets on the fight. So we got it on. It was the best fight in the history of Northern Michigan. We damn near killed each other, and we both ended up in the hospital. All the kids changed their bets—the first guy out of the hospital would be considered the winner. I made it out of the hospital first, eyes crossed. But it changed me a little bit because I learned you can't live forever. And there is always somebody out there who can turn you inside out, regardless of who you are or how tough you are.

My junior year brought more bad news. I couldn't stay healthy. My first stroke of bad luck occurred in practice, on the same day President John Kennedy was assassinated in 1963. I took an elbow in the side of the face, and it felt like I'd been hit by a car. The doctors said my salivary glands had been crushed, and they had to temporarily cut off my right ear and peel back my face to fix them. Before the surgery, they told me I would end up with a frozen face, that I'd never be able to smile. I'd look just like Chuck Noll. But after six hours, the surgeon came out and told my mother she should congratulate him, because he had just done one helluva job on her son.

I recovered, but things would only get worse. The following April, on the last play of the spring game, I suffered the worst hit of my life. I was playing outside linebacker, roughly where the strong safety would line up today. Right at the end of the play, after the whistle, the center for the white squad, Jerry Gorlitz, clipped me. The play was over, but he just hammered me in the legs. I never saw him. When I got hit, it torqued my left knee and snapped off the bottom of my femur. Frank Novak, a nifty quarterback who would later coach with us in Houston, won the game for the green squad. I got carried off in a Dodge station wagon.

The doctors really didn't know how to fix my knee. There was no way of getting in there and fixing it properly, like they do today with arthroscopic procedures. After all, this was close to thirty years ago. They told me, "That's it, you're through." I couldn't believe this was happening to me. I had never even given any thought to graduating from college. I was simply enjoying playing football. I still had no idea what I would do after college.

My injury bothered me so much I didn't even want to go to our games. I couldn't even sit in the stands. But Rollie Dotsch was a good man and a great coach. He knew I had a strong football mind, and he asked me to start scouting opponents. So, at the age of twenty, I limped around with a cane to see other teams play. And I started enjoying the hell out of writing those scouting reports every week. Rollie taught me that I could still enjoy the game without playing it. He taught me to use my mind, instead of my body. As a player, football had been seek and destroy. Now I was starting to think about matchups, looking for an opponent's weakness. It reminded me of my psychology classes. I loved it.

Rollie went on to be an assistant coach with the Green Bay Packers, the New England Patriots, the Detroit Lions, and of course, from 1977 to 1982, the Pittsburgh Steelers, where he earned two Super Bowl rings. (Later, when I became an assistant coach in the NFL, I actually coached against both my high school and college coaches. That's got to be an NFL first.) Every coach has his own ideas, and the foundation of my coaching career started with Rollie's philosophy.

"Let's get after it good," Rollie would say. "Take chances, but take calculated risks."

On defense, he was aggressive, a little bit unorthodox; he gave people some looks that were not widely recognized or accepted as sound. But I believed they were sound. And offensively, he insisted on a strong running game to go with the passing game. Not just the typical "you've got to run the football to be able to throw the football" bullcrap, but he wanted a running game that would dominate, overpower, even if you only needed it a few times a game.

"At one time or another," he'd say, "whether it's third and 1 or third and 12, there are times and situations when you have to run the ball and run it well."

That idea always sort of stuck with me.

Rollie finally became a head coach in the pros in 1983, when he took over the Birmingham Stallions of the United States Football League, where he worked until 1985. In 1986, he became an assistant coach with the Minnesota Vikings. During his stint with Minnesota, he went for a physical one day and found out he had colon cancer. The man was only fifty-five years old. From the time he found out he was sick, I called him every week, right up to the week he died. Several times I broke down and cried on the phone when we were talking. When he died in 1987, I was crushed, like a part of me had been ripped away.

I'll never forget Rollie Dotsch saying, "Hey, Jer, you can't play. But maybe you can do something else."

Yeah, Coach, just maybe. I had given some thought to coaching. Rollie Dotsch was the man who put wheels on my dreams.

The other day, I was flipping through my senior yearbook. The editor had written every senior's favorite phrase or verse next to their photo. Next to my picture was written:

"Life without football is not life."

That says it all.

3

Living on the Edge

When I got my first offer to coach football, I was working in a mill, lifting 100-pound bags of flour. When the Ohio high school system asked if I was interested in being an assistant coach, they didn't have to ask twice. That was in 1964. I was on my new job just a few days when I came to a conclusion that would be my trademark for the rest of my coaching career: I determined that while my players might not be the fastest, the strongest, or the biggest, they would be football players.

By that I mean physical. I wanted guys who would live on the edge, play the game the way it should be played; flying to the football, with devil-be-damned, knock-your-jock-off recklessness. I learned early that physical football wins games you shouldn't win. There's nothing like a savage, full-speed, *legal* hit, where the guy just *crumples* under the force of the blow, and you feel the fight go right out of him. Some guys just quit after a hit like that. I've seen the greatest players in the game "go in

25

the tank" after they've been tagged. But you *have* to play whistle to whistle. I believe that if you haven't heard a whistle, then there's room for one more helmet on the football.

So from the beginning, I wanted guys who would hit, hustle and chase. And even in high school, I found a few. It takes players willing to accept your philosophy and attitude, players who play hard for you. I've been fortunate that at every level, even high school, I've had players who liked black eyes and admired broken noses. It became our trademark.

I was sitting in my office one afternoon in 1966 when the phone rang. It was Rollie Dotsch from Northern Michigan.

"Jerry," he said, "I'm looking at some of your defensive game film."

Immediately, I thought he was recruiting two of our linebackers, who were undersized but would kill their own mothers to get to the football.

"Yeah, Coach, whatcha think of our youngsters?" I said proudly. "They really fly to the football, don't they? Which one do you want? I'll send him to you."

"Neither one," Rollie answered. "I want the guy coaching those guys to be that aggressive. There's only one guy I know who would coach what they're doing. And that's you. I've got linebackers. I want you."

I was speechless. For Rollie Dotsch to tell me that he thought enough of my coaching to hire me was the highest compliment I'd ever received.

"My staff is full right now," Rollie said, "but it's time

for you to get into college coaching. I'm going to recommend you to some people, so stay close to your phone."

The phone rang. And rang. Western Kentucky. Brown University. Small schools looking for a jolt to wake up their football programs.

I chose Western Kentucky.

Nick Dennis was Western's head coach in 1967. Joe Bugel, who's now the head coach of the Phoenix Cardinals, was hired to coach the entire offense. I was handed the entire defense. We had only four coaches, so each guy coached an entire unit at the same time. There was no tight end coach or linebacker coach, no "specialization" coaching like there is today. It was just us.

Joe and I moved in together, in a little log cabin near the campus. Obviously we weren't making much money, which meant we didn't always have food. We would eat real good right after a payday, but with about two weeks left in the month, we were down to scraps. We'd take two cans of food and stick them in boiling water, then eat the food out of the cans. But we learned football. I didn't have a car, but Joe did, and we would ride up and down I-75 together and visit every spring practice within driving distance. We were curious how everybody else coached. We were just two young guys trying to learn everything we could about football.

When Joe and I could afford pizza, we would take a big pizza home and spend the entire night drawing formations on the box. He'd design an offense, and I'd draw up a defense to stop him. We did more football on the bottom of pizza boxes than anywhere else. The next day, we would carry pizza boxes into meetings and show the other coaches. We invented things as we went along, and it worked. By the time the season started, we both were living on the edge. We called it "happy-hand-grenade football," just wide-open, get-after-you football. Occasionally Joe and I would disagree. We had incredible arguments. Two headstrong guys going head to head. One time we had a huge argument in the hallway outside the locker room, and next thing I knew, we were throwing punches. Joe was bleeding. I was bleeding. And not a single player dared interfere. They just watched, incredulously. They'd never seen two *coaches* beat the hell out of each other before. The fight lasted ten or fifteen minutes, then it sort of relapsed back into an argument, then it ended. And, of course, we remained friends. In fact, I like a guy more if he stands up and fights for himself and for what he believes.

On the first day of practice, I gathered the defense around me in a big circle and started coaching every position. It's tough to coach all eleven positions—the truth is, you can't. But we did the best we could.

"To hell with reading and reacting," I told them. "I want you to attack and force the issue. We want to maul people. We want everybody going after the football."

Years later, when I became defensive coordinator with the Atlanta Falcons, we called our defense the "Gritz Blitz," because we sent everybody after the quarterback. But few people realize the "Gritz Blitz" began at Western Kentucky in 1967. We did the exact same thing, and nobody had ever seen a football team be that aggressive.

We shut a lot of people out and gave up only a little more than 30 yards a game. We went undefeated, with one tie.

That year I completed my master's degree at Western Kentucky, and I have to admit it was one of the finest years of my life. Joe would leave Western the next year to become an assistant coach at Navy, and I would be moving on, too. But at Western, we never had a dull moment, even when we weren't coaching. During the spring, for instance, he taught first aid to women and I coached the women's bowling team and drove the bus.

"OK ladies," I'd tell my first-day bowlers, "let's get our minds out of the gutter."

At the end of the 1967–68 school year, I interviewed with Bud Carson, who then was head coach at Georgia Tech and is now head coach of the Cleveland Browns. Bud invited me down to Atlanta for a visit. At the time, he had an impossible situation. The Yellow Jackets hadn't recruited well in recent years. When we interviewed, we disagreed on a lot of things, basically, philosophy. But we were kindred spirits; hardheaded, stubborn and dirt tough. Bud hired me.

When I met the other assistant coaches, I knew we had a chance. These guys knew football, understood football. Bud knew how to hire a staff. he had Lamar Leachman, who is now the defensive line coach of the Detroit Lions, and Tom Moore, who is now the assistant head coach of the Minnesota Vikings. We didn't know we had four future NFL coaches on the staff.

At Georgia Tech, I lived about as far out there on the edge as a man can go. I had matured a little from my high school days, but my love for fast cars and motorcycles hadn't changed. I rode a black four-cylinder Honda to work every day. I rode that sucker into the ground. Every year I would take off by myself, ride all over the country, just for the thrill of it. Once I rode from Atlanta to Quebec, Canada, and stopped at La Château Frontenac, perhaps the classiest hotel in North America. I had on bib overalls, my hair had been under a helmet all day and I looked like the wrong end of a bad fight.

"Go away," the valet told me.

I showed him my reservation. He looked shocked.

"Uh, *forgive* me," the valet said.

You should have seen them try to valet park my motorcycle. On another long trip, I was sleeping on a roadside picnic table when a guy woke me up and demanded my money. I whipped out a 10-inch knife that I always carried with me and asked the guy if he had ever been stuck. And I offered to do it for no charge.

He declined. And left. Quickly.

Atlanta appealed to me, and I worked hard for Bud Carson. At Georgia Tech, they gave us Buick Rivieras to recruit with, and I wore out two cars a year. Sooner or later, my car would surrender. I'd drive 100 miles per hour all over north Georgia, Tennessee, Kentucky and Ohio. My car would quit, and I would call Bud and tell him I needed more money or another car. This was the good ol' days, before all these NCAA sanctions and recruiting restrictions. We could sign whoever we wanted to sign. There was no limit. We signed maybe sixty-five or seventy guys a year. If you were breathing and looked like an athlete, we gave you a shot. We signed everybody in the hope that twenty-two of them would be able to play football. And it worked.

Under Bud's direction, we started winning and went to three bowl games in five years. By my fourth year there, I was getting phone calls, job offers, *good* job offers. I couldn't believe it. George Allen called me and offered me a job with the Redskins. But I didn't want to go. I told George thanks, but no thanks, because it would take a perfect situation before I would leave Bud.

During this time, I lived in a singles-only apartment complex. For two years, I'd noticed that I had a darn good-looking next-door neighbor, but during the season I always came home real late and during the off-season I was always recruiting. But occasionally we'd see each other and exchange smiles. Finally one day I asked her out. Her name was Brenda, and she had long brown hair and long legs. She was going to night school at Georgia State at the time. We started dating, and she made it to a few games. After one game, a particularly tough loss, Brenda offered her first, and last, opinion on coaching.

Let's get one thing straight here. I hate losing. Some coaches say, "Well, we can learn from losing." I'd personally rather learn from winning. When I lose at anything, it makes me want to vomit. So after this loss, Brenda and I were riding in the car, down I-75, and the tension was just a bit thick.

"Jerry," she said softly, "it's only a game. Why do you take a game so seriously?"

I locked the brakes, which nearly put Brenda through the windshield. Everything in the seats was thrown all over the car. I pulled over on the side of the interstate.

"If you honestly feel like that, then get out of my car right now," I bellowed, eyes blazing. "It's not a *stupid* game. It's my *life*, for God's sake."

Brenda, a soft-spoken and extremely shy girl, looked at me with horror. She had only been trying to console me. But she got the picture. Life is fun. Being employed in football is fun. But losing never has been and never will be fun. That's the only time I don't have a sense of humor.

To this day, I feel bad for my outburst. I was a jackass. But Brenda never again did any more coaching. Which, in my opinion, made her extra special.

In 1974, Rick Forzano offered me a job with the Detroit Lions as special teams coach. I respected Rick Forzano. I had met him at an NCAA coaches convention when he was the head coach at Navy, where he had recruited and coached a guy named Roger Staubach. Joe Bugel introduced us. At first, I didn't want to go. At the time, there weren't many special teams coaches in the NFL. I called Rick.

"Coach, I'm not coming," I said. "I just don't feel that being special teams coach is much of a responsibility."

"Hey, baby," Rick said, "you're making a big mistake. If you want to get into the NFL, this is your chance.

Coaching special teams is just as important as being an offensive or defensive coordinator. The job is only what you make out of it."

That changed my mind. Bud Carson had taken a job with the Pittsburgh Steelers, so I felt no obligation to hang around at Georgia Tech. Besides, it was my boyhood dream to go back and coach with the Lions. I had just built a brand-new home in Georgia, and I hated leaving. But I stuck the For Sale sign in the yard and headed north to Detroit.

Rick had assembled a great staff in Detroit. My old buddy Joe Bugel was the offensive line coach, Raymond Berry worked with receivers, Fritz Shurmur coached the defensive line, Jimmy Carr coached defensive backs and Bill Belichick helped with the defense. It may have been one of the finest staffs ever assembled. Rick was big on teaching. He showed me that you can't just order guys around, you have to teach them *why* you do certain things. He always had the right answer, always made great decisions. And he believed like I did: On defense, you hit anything that moves.

Rick was big on discipline. He wanted all his coaches wearing ties. I hate ties. So I wore a bolo tie. He didn't care for my motorcycle, either. I was still riding my Honda motorcycle to work in Detroit; the only difference was that I had to chain it to a light pole. One year, right before the season started, I had taken one of my usual cross-country rides. When I reported back to the Lions, Rick was waiting on me.

"I'm glad to see you," he said. "I was worried that I'd

be scooping you off the highway somewhere with a shovel. You always have to be different, don't you?"

But when it came to coaching, we were together. Rick was demanding, he wanted 110 percent from his coaches. We were both in love with a projector and football. One night when we were watching film we came up with an expression—NHPA, which stood for "No Hustle Play Away." In other words, we'd see guys standing around watching when the play went the other way. We didn't want those guys. We wanted guys who hustled from whistle to whistle.

For the next three years, we coached the craziest, hardest-hitting special teams in football. I recommended to Rick another young assistant coach named Floyd Reese, who later would end up coaching our linebackers at Houston. Back then I worked with linebackers and special teams. Floyd and I hit it off—he believed in broken noses, too. Once again, we got after people. The schemes we came up with for special teams are the exact schemes we're still using today. We wanted full-speed collisions, guys who would explode into the wedge and make people pay a price for carrying the football.

We also loved to block kicks. We found eleven of the nastiest guys in America and put them on the punt-block team, and we set an NFL record for most blocked punts in a season, with five. And we came close a hundred times. Punters seldom had good days against us, because they were too worried about the block—and themselves. Because a lot of times when we blocked the punt, we drilled the guy kicking the ball. By pure accident, of course. We *worked* on special teams every single day. We spent hours blocking extra points. We taught our troops that special teams could, and should, score points. If a guy wouldn't give us 100 percent, we didn't want him. But if a guy made a big hit, I'd be the first guy to run and hug him. Games can change on special teams. To this day, I still believe that.

One night in Detroit, all the coaches were watching film when we came up with the idea of using an eleven-man front on defense. Just line up all eleven defensive guys on the football and send them after the quarterback. Now this was not conventional thinking. But we didn't have the greatest talent at Detroit. When you have a lot of talent, you can line up in a basic 4–3 defense and just sit back and play. But Rick taught me that when you're getting blood out of a turnip, you have to put doubt in the minds of the other guys.

Jimmy Carr, who everybody called "Gummy" because he had false teeth, named our eleven-man front "Sticky Sam." It confused the hell out of a lot of people. One time we were playing Green Bay, and John Hadl was their quarterback. We must have sacked him eight times. We lined up in our Sticky Sam defense thirty-four times. One time he came out of the huddle, just after we'd drilled him again, and we lined up with eleven guys on the line of scrimmage.

"Not again," Hadl said. Then he called time out.

After two seasons in Detroit I was still going back to Atlanta a lot during the off-season to see Brenda. Finally

I caught her at a weak moment and asked her to marry me. It took her forever to say yes. I found this certain church in Atlanta and insisted we get married there. When General Sherman had marched through Atlanta during the Civil War, only two buildings were left standing. A little Catholic church, and a building next to it where they stabled their horses. I figured if this church could survive the Civil War, it could survive my marriage. So we got married in the stable where General Sherman had once stabled his horse. I thought that was appropriate for an old mule like me.

Brenda and I went back to Detroit for my third season with Rick Forzano, but he resigned after four games in 1976, after two back-to-back 7–7 seasons. We stuck out the year under new head coach Tommy Hudspeth, but it wasn't the same without Rick. Under Rick, we won games that we shouldn't have won. Guys played over their heads. We didn't have the personnel. But because we didn't win a lot, Rick became the scapegoat. That's the way it is in the NFL. We did a lot of innovative things in Detroit. But fans only care if you win. You can go 12–0 and tell everybody, "Our whole team wore two left shoes," and the next year the entire league will wear two left shoes. But if you go 7–7, nobody gives a darn about anything you did.

So I started listening to offers for other jobs. Tommy Prothro wanted me in San Diego. Red Miller offered me a job in Denver. New England called. But I kept hoping that something would work out in Atlanta. Leeman Bennett, who at one time had been an assistant to Rick

Forzano, had become the head coach in Atlanta, and Rick suggested to both of us that we talk. We finally did, and in 1977, I ended up as the special teams and defensive backs coach of the Atlanta Falcons. At the time, they were one of the worst teams in football. I find it funny that every time I'm unemployed, only the bad teams want me. My whole career I've received cards and letters from the best teams in football, telling me "good job," "great improvement," "excellent work." But every time I've needed a job, I've never heard from those guys.

But I was glad to be going to Atlanta, for several reasons. First, Brenda's parents lived there, and she liked being close to home. And second, my house, the one I'd built during my last season with Georgia Tech, still hadn't sold. So we took down the For Sale sign and just moved back in.

Leeman was a unique coach. He turned his back on his assistants and let them do whatever they had to do to get the job done. His only concern was the score at the end of the game. So we went crazy. Doug Shively, who later would coach for me at Houston and now in Atlanta again, was coaching the linebackers. We drew up some crazy defenses that looked a lot like the old Sticky Sam formation we ran at Detroit. We had lived on the edge in Detroit, but in Atlanta, we inched out there just a little bit further.

In 1977, we opened up at home against the Los Angeles Rams. We were the worst team in the NFL, and they were the division champions and had a quarterback named Joe Namath. Leeman didn't care what we did, just as long as we won. So we called the safety blitz forty-six times in that game. I told my defensive backs that while I *preferred* they hit Namath while he still had the ball, just hit him. You nail any quarterback enough times and, sooner or later, throwing touchdowns will be the last thing on his mind. All quarterbacks, even Joe Namath, will eventually say, "Screw this, I'm too young to die."

But early in the game, Namath was still Namath. On one play he read the blitz and hit a post-corner route for a touchdown. But there was a flag on the play, and the touchdown was called back. On the next down, Namath called the same play, we called the same blitz. We nailed him again, but he hit the same post-corner route for a touchdown. That made us mad, so we kept blitzing. We sent cornerbacks, safeties, linebackers, even a few ball boys—me and Shive were sending everybody. Namath still had the arm, but he couldn't run. He stood there like his feet were stuck in cement and took a real beating. We won the game, 17–6.

After the game, poor Joe couldn't move. On the airplane back to Los Angeles, he had the Rams trainers pack him in ice. The reporters gathered around us after the game—they'd never seen such ridiculous, all-out blitzing in their lives.

"What the hell was that?"

"You just saw the Gritz Blitz, baby," I said.

A monster was born. The fans booed if we didn't blitz on every down. We rallied around the Gritz Blitz all season and gave up just 129 points in fourteen games, then an NFL record. We also intercepted a club-record twenty-six passes, because quarterbacks were just throwing and ducking. Our defense that year gave up less than 100 yards passing *per game*, which might be the best in history. We finished just 7–7, however, which taught me that if and when I ever became a head coach, I'd take the same chances on offense. You don't take chances, you don't get anywhere in life. There are a lot of talented people in the NFL who are afraid to get creative because if it doesn't work, people say nasty things about your mother. But when you live on the edge, you have to be able to take the heat. And it doesn't hurt to have a mother with thick skin.

In Atlanta we found guys who would play on the edge, like safeties Tom Pridemore and Bob Glazebrook. I don't believe in cheap shots. But if you're playing aggressive football, you're going to hit late occasionally. And I hate guys who run out of bounds—sidelines are for college players. Just go get the guy with the ball. Punish him for having it. And tell him you'll see him on the next play.

Some guys couldn't take it. Like George Rogers of the New Orleans Saints, who accused our team of late-hit football. I hate when people call us dirty. George wasn't willing to play at our level, he wasn't willing to *earn* his paycheck. Ask Namath, who despite the whipping we gave him, was quick to say that we weren't dirty, only physical.

In Atlanta, we came up with the Iwo Jima philosophy. On every play, we wanted to put up the flag. We had everybody tackling the football, diving, flying, jumping on the ballcarrier. Everybody wanted their shot. Once

Bob Glazebrook dove into a pile and broke the upper arm of defensive end Jeff Merrow. After Jeff healed, Glazebrook asked him for the X ray and the cast of his arm.

"I want to frame them and put them over my mantel," Glaze said. "It's the first broken arm I've ever done, even if it is my own teammate."

I love pro football. Glaze was my kind of guy.

On March 9, 1979, Leeman Bennett named me the defensive coordinator of the Falcons.

"Jerry," he told me, "you've been calling all the defensive signals anyway, so you may as well get the title."

But when I was an assistant coach, I never cared about titles. I cared about responsibilities. Too many assistant coaches spend so much time trying to become head coaches that they quit being good assistant coaches. I always tried to be the best damn assistant coach I could be, in hopes that somebody would make me a head coach. I'd learned from guys like Rick Forzano, Bud Carson and Leeman Bennett that being a good coach meant getting through to your people. Putting things in the right language. Making good decisions.

In Atlanta we won a lot of games on the last play. And our quarterback, Steve Bartkowski, won a lot of games for us. In 1980 we were 12–4, and Bart saved our butts a hundred times. He was a pressure quarterback. If the defense gave up a big play, he'd come back with two of his own. We started seven rookies on defense, including a defensive back named Kenny Johnson.

"The only guys you like, Coach," Kenny told me once, "are trained killers. Like me."

He was right. Our trained killers won the division and made the playoffs against Dallas. That was a crusher. Dallas beat us on three long bombs from Danny White. He got hammered on all three touchdowns, and all three passes were jump balls. Their receivers just pulled them down. You didn't see us in the Super Bowl, but we were the best team in the NFL that year. No excuses—we just didn't play well that day.

After the 1982 season, Leeman Bennett was fired. It was time for me to move on. I spent a short season in Buffalo as secondary coach, then in 1984 Hugh Campbell, who had been named head coach of the Oilers, offered me a job as Houston's defensive coordinator. It took me about five seconds to figure out that Houston was a lot warmer than Buffalo.

My first day there, we greeted the defense. Our work was cut out for us. You can't judge a jockey until you see him on the horse, and you can't judge a defense until you see it in the game. But these guys didn't seem too excited.

"Fellas," I said, "we'll do some hitting soon. If the Houston Oilers are ever going to make the playoffs, we're gonna have to find out who our trained killers are."

4

The Man in Black

Winning football begins with attitude. Which is a darn good thing, because when I took the job in Houston as defensive coordinator in 1984, we didn't have many players. The year before I arrived, the Oilers gave up 460 points, good for twenty-seventh among twenty-eight teams. They were the worst defense in the NFL against the run and sacked the quarterback only thirty-one times.

Defenses get beat by mental errors. I don't believe you win a game with cerebral ideas. Your players have to know what they're doing. They have to react, not think. So we set out to simplify things. And, of course, we set out to find some trained killers. But killer instinct begins with the players, and that was a problem.

In 1984, the Oilers had some guys who were really good boys with the nicest mommies and daddies you ever met. But they wouldn't hit anybody if you gave 'em a stick and leaked on their boots. When I first took a good look at Houston's personnel that year, I knew we were

42

in a whole lot of trouble. We had a lot of older guys who
were at the end of their careers. They still looked
mean, like an old huntin' dog, but their huntin' days
were over.

"I'll be sick if we don't start hitting people," I said.
"We will *not* be a bend-but-don't-break defense. There
won't be any eighteen-play drives. They may score, but
it won't take eighteen plays. We're gonna pin our ears
back and start smacking people."

Guys looked around the room like I was crazy. Which
is okay, because I am. Back then, the Oilers held training camp in San Angelo, Texas, and it was ideal. The
conditions were so bad, so nasty, that we didn't have to
cut the wimps. The wimps went home on their own. The
temperatures soared past 100 degrees every day, sometimes hovering around 110 or 115 degrees. A reporter
from KSAT-TV in San Antonio used a parking lot curb
to fry an egg and then ate it on the air. It was like playing
football in hell. One afternoon it had to be close to 120
degrees. Guys were just reeling from the heat. We looked
up at the end of a midmorning practice and the sun *and*
moon were both visible overhead. Jeff Parks, a rookie
tight end from Auburn, pointed to the sky and cried out,
"Oh my God, everybody, we've got just seventeen hours
to live."

The heat was so bad we couldn't tape the players'
names on their helmets—the tape melted.

"But if I do something good, how will you know it was
me?" one of the rookies asked me.

"Believe me, kid," I said, "if anybody here does anything right, we *will* remember. And if I don't know your name, I'll ask to see your driver's license."

"But I'm a *game* player, Coach," the kid argued. "I can't practice in this heat."

"Don't save anything for the prom, sweetheart," I replied, "because you might not get asked to go."

Improving the Oilers was like eating an elephant. We had to do it one bite at a time. The players began to absorb our philosophy, which is simple: Hit to the whistle. If there's seven helmets on the ball, let's get eight. If there's nine helmets on the ball, let's get ten. If there's eleven helmets on the ball, and you're near our sideline, what the hell, let's get twenty. That's called a "stand-up defense," because when that many people just crush the ballcarrier, the crowd stands up.

We like that.

We improved a little on defense, but I'll be honest— my first two seasons in Houston were not pretty. Head coach Hugh Campbell had been quite a coach in the Canadian Football League, where the playing fields are about the size of Texas. Hugh's big thing was offense. Back then, I spent every second of my time on defense. The only thing I really remember about our offense was that every time I looked out on the field, our quarterback was getting sacked. But it's hard to blame one side of the ball. We were just a terrible football team. There's no other way to say it. If we had been a college team, everybody would've scheduled us for homecoming.

This was one time in my life when I completely lost my sense of humor. At one point, we lost ten games in a row. Those are tough times—but I'm convinced it made me a better coach. We tried to work our way out of it. But working more hours can't compensate for the guys you're lining up with. We finally broke our losing streak, against Kansas City, with a familiar tactic—we blitzed them every single play for four quarters. Then we won three out of our last six to finish the year.

But Hugh's relationship with the front office was still very tense in 1985, especially after we lost five in a row. It's tough to live and work day to day. We kept waiting for the hammer to fall. Finally it happened. Only the end result wasn't quite what I anticipated.

We had just been beaten up by the New York Giants, with two games to play—the year before New York would go to the Super Bowl. I went in to work on Monday, and then–personnel director Mike Holovak met me the second I stepped off the elevator. He took me down the hall to see Ladd Herzeg, the general manager, who motioned for me to sit down. By the time Ladd started to talk, I was humming "These Boots Were Made for Walkin'." I knew I was about to be fired.

"Jerry," Ladd said, "I want you to take over the team as the head coach, at least for the next two games."

I couldn't believe it. I wasn't even aware that Hugh had already been fired. Instantly, I got a mixed reaction. Sick to my stomach. When a coach gets fired, it isn't just him that didn't get the job done. There's a lot of other coaches and players involved. But you can't fire forty-five players.

"No," I stammered, "I can't do it."

Holovak and Herzeg looked at each other.

"But Hugh is already gone," Ladd said.

"If I don't take the job," I asked, "is there any way I would be considered for the head coaching job *next* year?"

Both men shook their heads no.

"If you take the interim job, we promise you'll be considered for next season," Herzeg said. "If you win the last two games, you positively will be hired for next year."

That's called lathering you up before they shave you. The last two games were on the road. At the time, the Oilers had won only four road games in five years. But nevertheless, on December 10, 1985, I was named the head coach of the Houston Oilers.

Before I met the press, I decided I should wear a necktie. I hate ties. They give me a rash. But I decided that I should dress up for this occasion, because it might not ever happen again. So I called my wife and asked her to bring me a coat and tie for the announcement. I have one tie that has a picture of a dog watering a fire hydrant. I thought seriously about wearing that one, but decided to save it for my first trip to Cleveland. Brenda brought down the tie that I wore when I got married, which was exactly the last time I'd worn a tie.

So we mugged for the cameras and answered questions. When I took the job, I really didn't feel any pressure. I just set out to do the best job I possibly could. My theory is simple: No matter what happens with football, I have the best wife and son in the world. I have a dog that'll still hunt. I have a car that's down to thirty-six payments. And I belong to one helluva church. If I get fired today, I'm better off than most people.

The media wanted to know if the "personality" of the team would change. I made that clear from the very beginning. "We're gonna knock people down," I said. "We're not going to trick you or finesse you. But every player today wears a cage, a face mask, on his helmet. We're gonna show people why. We will be living on the edge."

The transformation didn't happen overnight—I didn't have a magic wand. We played hard but lost our last two games, at Cleveland and Indianapolis, and Herzeg started the long process of looking for a full-time replacement. The list was long. Dick Coury of the Los Angeles Rams. Paul Hackett of the San Francisco 49ers. Tom Osborne at Nebraska. They even interviewed me a few times. The *Houston Post* ran a readers' poll to see who the fans wanted, and Hackett was the hands-down favorite.

Herzeg asked me what I would do if I stayed.

"That's simple," I told him. "We'll be better my first year. And we'll be in the playoffs every year after that. Period."

For some strange reason, they kept me around. The first guy I hired was Doug Shively, who had been with me at Atlanta with the Falcons. Then we got Floyd Reese, who had been in Minnesota. We pieced together a good staff, a staff that believed in football the same way I do. One thing I didn't do was name an offensive or defensive coordinator. If somebody was gonna get blamed for a bad play, it would be me. If somebody got fired for bad coaching, it wouldn't be the offensive coordinator or defensive coordinator, it would be me. That's the way it's always been since I've been head coach. And I think my staff works harder than any staff in the NFL. I'll stand up for my staff. It's too easy for some head coaches to sacrifice their staffs every year, while they keep working. If my staff goes, I'm going. The point is, *I* hired these guys. Nobody else. Blame me.

Another thing we put an end to was the "reading and reacting" garbage that you read about so much in pro football today. I believe in setting the pace and then seeing if the other team can keep up. I told our coaches that our football team would go 100 miles per hour for four quarters—wide-open, smash-face football. I wanted to build a team that could throw effectively, but could also line up and run Mike Rozier over right guard six times in a row and bloody your nose.

Our biggest problem in 1986 was personnel. As a head coach, you have to be very, very careful that you don't think you are the reason that you're winning. It takes a whole lot of good people—good coaches and good players—to win a game in this league. In 1986, we set out to get some warm bodies that could play. And get rid of the ones who couldn't. There were plenty of those left. We had a tight end who told me that he would prefer not to do much blocking.

"I don't mind blocking, as long as I'm not running right at the guy," he explained. "I'm a better blocker when I can sneak up on somebody."

I'd never seen a 250-pound tight end sneak up on *anybody*. I wasn't smart enough to design an offense to help this guy. But he wasn't the worst one. We had running backs who would run out of bounds rather than bang it up inside for an extra yard. When they did run inside, they ran with their eyes closed. Our offensive line hated our backs worse than our opponents' defense. Our backs would just close their eyes and go, run right up the backs of the offensive linemen. Our linemen had cleat marks all over their backs.

"Jeez, Coach," Mike Munchak said one day, after he'd been smeared again by the same back. "Can't we just ask him to run *through* the holes?"

We also had the slowest wide receivers in the NFL. Our whole division had turned into a bump-and-run, man-to-man conference, and here we were with the slowest receivers in the league. They all had real nice families and nice parents, but they couldn't play football.

We had one guy with a pet snake. He was a big hit on kids' day, the kids absolutely loved him and the snake. We cut him, and my son, Justin, said, "Dad, can you cut him and keep the snake?" That snake added three years to his career. We made it clear to our players from the first day that times were changing. We told them we'd rather be known as a staff with teams that played hard than a staff that made a lot of friends. We wanted effort. We wanted all-out hustle. And most of all, we wanted courage, guys who would volunteer to throw their bodies on a live hand grenade.

The Oilers had a good draft that year, but at the time,

nobody realized it. They got wide receiver Ernie Givens and running back Allen Pinkett, and then in the middle rounds, picked up linebackers Robert Lyles and Johnny Meads, two guys, who are still the soul of Houston's defense. The Oilers brought back a bunch of skill people like Mike Rozier and Drew Hill. The offensive line had guys like Dean Steinkuhler, Bruce Matthews and Mike Munchak. Center Jay Pennison signed as a free agent.

So we had a good nucleus to build with. Now we just had to change their attitudes and get the young guys some experience. I reminded the team about a game at Pittsburgh in 1985, when one of their linemen jumped offsides, picked up our quarterback, turned him upside down and drove him into the turf. Everybody just stood and watched while our QB lay there with his eyes rolled back in his head. No one helped him or fought for him. Nothing. It was embarrassing.

I'd never seen a team mistreat another team the way Pittsburgh mistreated us in the early eighties. Look at the film. We'd be down by 40 and they're still blitzing, still killing our running backs, still punching our guys in the mouth, still jumping offsides and crushing our quarterback for no reason. They were the most physical, vile team I'd ever seen. I vowed that they would never treat us like that again.

"Guys, no more of this 'be-intelligent-if-they-hit-you-don't-hit-them-back' bull," I said. "For the past two years, we've been 'smart,' and we haven't punched back. And we have the bruises to show for it. From now on, if they hit you, I want *the entire team* hitting back. If they hit one of ours, we *will* come back and protect him. If you want respect, you have to start standing up to people."

We had to convince our team: We're not here to play the game, we're here to win the game. And to win, we had to start living on the edge. Throw deep on first down. Knock the stuffing out of people. Block punts. Go crazy. If they hit you, hit them back. When I took over the Oilers, nobody had job security. Not me, not my assistant coaches, not the players. We simply didn't have the time to rebuild with a bunch of nice guys—we'd all be fired. So we had to find a way to win immediately.

Chuck Noll never complained about the Houston Oilers until we beat him twice in the same season. But Chuck deserves the credit for turning Houston around. He probably had more to do with us becoming a winning football team than I did. His total disrespect for the Oilers did more to change our attitudes than anything else, and for that, I thank him.

You can't be an aggressive football team without some aggressive penalties. We can live with those and win with those. The penalties that beat you are backward penalties, like false start, illegal motion, offsides. Those give me heartburn.

Going into my first preseason as a head coach, I made a decision that would create more hoopla than any single thing I've ever done. I decided to wear black on the sidelines. For several reasons. One, because it's my favorite color; all my cars are black on black. Two, because it helped players spot me from the field. When a player's standing on the 50-yard line and looks toward the bench, all he sees is a maze. I planned to make some of the decisions on penalties and play calls. When the players looked toward the bench, I didn't want them wasting their time, straining their eyes looking for the short guy.

Black also makes a statement, it sets a tone. Of course, the media and opposing fans and players taunted me for wearing black. But some of our players liked it, and that's what counted. Too much was made out of the "man in black." The bottom line is that a coach can't dominate a game. I've never seen a coach make a tackle or run the football or catch a touchdown. But if it motivated our players, then it's worth it. Slowly but surely, we were making rebels out of everybody. We won only five games my first year, but we lost four games by a total of 15 points and two more in overtime. We were on the brink of being a good football team.

We continued to get rid of the guys who wouldn't put out. We had a big, lazy offensive lineman named Harvey Salem who looked like Tarzan but played like Jane. First he missed camp over some technicality in his contract. Then when he finally reported, all he did was complain and moan and groan. Guys like that can tear down everything you're trying to build up. One day I just couldn't take any more. I took all of his gear out of his locker— shoulder pads, helmet, pants, jersey, everything—and put it into a toilet stall. Then I put his nameplate over the stall.

He came in, and he stormed around like a big old

cow. We told him that if he wanted to dress for practice, he'd have to dress in the commode. He stormed out and demanded to be traded. And he had the nerve to request a team on the coast. "Trade me anywhere, as long as it's on the water," Harvey said. So we did. We put him right on the water—Detroit, where he could enjoy the lovely breeze blowing off the Detroit River.

In 1987, the players went on strike and we played three games without them. But we finished 9–6 and made the playoffs and beat Seattle at home in the wild-card game. We got a lot better that year because we brought in two more assistant coaches on offense, two guys named June Jones and Kim Helton. Shively recommended Kim Helton, a former center for the University of Florida, as an offensive line coach. Kim and I see eye to eye on a few things: He hates losers, and he hates cowards. Kim really improved our running game, especially in passing situations.

June was another story. He was the backup quarterback when I was with the Atlanta Falcons, and when we worked out the secondary, June ran the scout team. He had a pitiful arm, but an inquisitive mind. He always was asking questions. He probably watched the defense more than the offense. He had also played under Mouse Davis at Portland State, running the run 'n' shoot offense. The run 'n' shoot is a passing offense that spreads the field with four wide receivers. Mouse and June both believe the pass should set up the run, not the other way around.

Mouse and June had been in Houston in 1984, with the Houston Gamblers of the USFL. They threw the ball fifty times a game, and Jim Kelly set a professional record with 5,219 yards passing. That offense made Jim Kelly famous. I knew June well, and I knew we could use his unpredictability on offense. So much of the NFL is boring. It's run on first down. Run on second. Pass on third. We wanted to be nonpredictable, nonconformists. If we're backed up on the goal line, let's hum-babe that ball out of there.

That's how we started using the "Red Gun" offense, the same four-receiver offense we use so much today. June would've run the offense full time, but I still believe in being unpredictable, being aggressive and using the clock. So we took the best of the run 'n' shoot and combined it with good, hard, smash-mouth running. We coached offense the same way we coached defense: wild and aggressive. Down and distance means nothing to us. We're gonna run a play that we like, with no regard for where the chains are.

In 1987, we walked close to the edge. Which made a lot of people mad, because we weren't supposed to be winning games. For years, the Oilers had been an automatic win on the schedule. That quickly changed. Against New Orleans, one of our linebackers, Walter Johnson, buried their kicker, Morten Andersen, on the opening kickoff. The suggestion came from our strength coach, Steve Watterson. At the time, Andersen was the most accurate kicker in the NFL. He had won half of the

Saints' games for them in the last minute. So we gave Morten a little wake-up call on the opening kickoff. We didn't go after his legs. We didn't go after his head. We wanted a good, clean, legal shot in the chest. And we got a legal hit. We didn't mean to break his ribs. But he did miss a couple field goals and kicked his next kickoff out of bounds.

We play physical football, whether we're winning by 30 or losing by 54. There have been a lot of easy riders in the NFL who didn't last long. That's why NFL stands for "Not For Long." But if you want to be around a while, you have to make your own rules, set your own limits and be tough enough to live with them. We just set our limits a little further out than a lot of people.

Cincinnati head coach Sam Wyche, who played for me at Detroit, was shocked after the New Orleans incident. He told me he couldn't believe we hit a kicker.

"Sam," I said, "I can't believe you'd say that. You played on our Detroit teams back when we used to have to *protect* our kicker."

In the 1960s and '70s, hitting the kicker was routine. So you assigned a man to protect him on the kickoff. But today kickers wear a lot of lipstick and try not to get their skirts dirty.

When we made the playoffs, it was the first time the Oilers had been there since 1980. The players were proud, and rightfully so. We had fought, scratched, clawed our way back into respectability in the NFL. "I think it's pretty obvious," tight end Jamie Williams said.

"We're the mutts of the league. The last of the wretched refuse. We've been knocked down so many times, it's ridiculous. But we keep on fighting."

The 1987 season was a great accomplishment for the Houston Oilers. It got them over the edge, proved they could win. Our quarterback threw more touchdowns in 1987 (twenty-one) than any Oiler since George Blanda in 1963. The same year, Houston also drafted the best fullback in football in Alonzo Highsmith. And when Tony Zendejas hit a winning field goal in overtime against Seattle, it was Houston's first home playoff victory ever.

Denver beat us in the second round of the playoffs. But people had learned to respect us. We made up our minds that in 1988 we would just teeter on the edge. We wanted to hang on the edge by our fingernails. We didn't care if people didn't like us. They're not supposed to. The media hated us. But we kept on winning and kept on smiling. People asked me all the time if all the controversy, all the criticism bothered me. Heck no, and I mean that still today. Life is too short. The average life span is what—about seventy years? The average NFL coaching career is only about four years. That's way too short to worry. I've never had a bad day in my life. Every day of my life, I've been lucky, I've been happy. I should start charging people 25 cents just to rub up against me.

When you live on the edge, some people love you and some people hate you.

But I wouldn't have it any other way. No apologies.

5

Hit the Beach

By 1988, the Oilers were finally a team, not a group of individuals. They had an attitude and a purpose. Somebody asked me then if we were just "trying to get even" with people in 1988, trying to pay back all the people who had stomped on us in previous years. The answer is no. I don't believe in getting even. Getting even means you're even, and that's not good enough. We want to beat you. Physically and on the scoreboard. But it only counts when we win. We've beaten people physically and lost the game.

The longer you are in the NFL, the more you learn to enjoy a win. A win is a win. In 1988, Houston struggled like crazy to beat New England, 7–6. Ladd Herzeg came up to me after the game.

He said, "That was the ugliest win I ever saw." Then he walked away in disgust.

Well, that ugly win put us in the playoffs three months later. Pete Rozelle didn't call the Houston Oilers and say, "That was an ugly win, it doesn't count in the stand-ings." There are no weak sisters in the NFL. Every team can beat you. And there's no such thing as a beautiful loss.

But what made 1988 so special was the arrival of our special teams. That year we hired a thirty-three-year-old special teams coach named Richard Smith, who had been coaching at the University of Arizona. Now, the way we hired coaches in Houston wasn't like everybody else. When we brought in a coach for an interview, every coach on the staff interviewed him. Then we all voted. Usually, the guy with the most votes got the job.

This time, we interviewed eight candidates for special teams. Richard didn't get any votes. But I liked the guy. First of all, he was just wacked. Crazy. And he had that boola-boola enthusiasm that you get in college. We already had the best special teams scheme in football. What we were looking for was somebody who was physically and mentally tough. And somebody who could bring incredible spirit to the guys on special teams.

We interviewed Richard for ninety minutes. He began every response with, "That's perfect." Or, "Perfect, simply perfect." I overruled the staff for the first time and hired him. To this day, Richard is called "Perfect" by the players and coaches.

"Perfect," I told him, "I want you to find eleven guys with suicidal tendencies. I want eleven guys who would throw themselves on a live hand grenade if we asked them to. Our special teams have to set the pace for the team. We don't want kickoffs and punts to be something you do between offense and defense. We want to score points, crush people, on kickoffs."

Perfect got this crazy gleam in his eyes, and they sort of rolled back in his head for a second.

"Coach," he said softly, "that'll be *perfect.*"

Perfect *was* perfect for special teams. In 1987, we were next to last in our conference in punt coverage and kickoff coverage. In 1988, we finished in the top five in the NFL. We also blocked five punts, which tied an NFL record set by my Detroit Lions' and Atlanta Falcons' special teams.

Perfect went out and found eleven crazy guys, just like we asked him to. He invented "over the top," where each week he would select one guy who would scream down the field and dive over the top of the other team's wedge. There were very few teams who enjoyed returning kickoffs against us.

We gave the special teams players nicknames. Jeff Donaldson, our strong safety, became "Lethal Weapon," for his head-on collisions. Keith Bostic became "Norman Bates," because he was psycho. Linebacker Eugene Seale, who someone said eats live rats, became "The One-Man Gang." In one season, Seale had eighteen solo tackles, blocked two punts and forced two fumbles. Against the Redskins, Seale knocked out return man Derrick Shephard.

One day Perfect walked into a special teams meeting wearing an army helmet.

"Uh-oh," I thought. "We really have pushed him over

the edge." On the front of the helmet was a skull and crossbones. On the other side was an Oiler logo. I tried to imagine Tom Landry wearing this helmet.

"Guys," he said, "every week, we will give out an army helmet just like this one to the guy who gets the best hit on special teams. The player who wins the helmet will wear it out on the field for the next game."

Eugene Seale won the first one, and he reluctantly wore it out on the field. The crowd roared. Seale turned and saluted the fans. Instantly, the helmet was a matter of pride. Everybody wanted to get a hit on special teams so they could get one. Perfect began calling our special teams "Hit the Beach," recalling the Allies' invasion of Normandy in World War II. *Veterans* began volunteering for special teams, which had to be a first for most of today's prima-donna players.

Kenny Johnson is a good example of a special teams player. He doesn't dodge people. he doesn't veer. He is a human missile. He runs right through you. We have a saying—no fair dodging. We don't want you to run down there in high heels and a purse. Some NFL teams can't find one or two guys who enjoy full-speed contact. In Houston, we had eleven, with at least that many more waiting in line for a chance.

Special teams are the most important part of football. They start the game, whether you win the toss or lose the toss. They can set the tempo faster than anything. They let the enemy know what's coming for the rest of the day. On the teams I coach, every day we ask the Lord to bless our players with the gift of hustle and the gift of courage.

We put those two things above ability and talent. We don't care what round you were drafted in, or where you went to school. If you hustle and you have great courage, you have a chance on our team.

Special teams rubbed off on the defense. And defense rubbed off on the offense. Pretty soon, we had everybody hitting anything that moved. Offensive linemen, defensive linemen, fullbacks, safeties, even kickers. We labeled big hits by the way they sounded. We had the "splat," which means the guy was just splattered out real good. A splat is hard to define; it's sort of like a bug hitting a windshield at 100 miles per hour. *That's* a splat. Somebody told me that they paid $30 to see a Mike Tyson fight on closed-circuit TV. I told them if they really wanted to see heads roll, pay $20 and come watch Houston's special teams.

Our Houston meetings turned into cheering sessions. We'd watch film, and when somebody got a big hit, the whole room went berserk. We'd run it back ten or fifteen times. Guys would hoot and holler, bang tables, stomp their feet. Our football team just oozed enthusiasm. We even went crazy when somebody splatted us. We especially like "window-shade" hits, where guys just flop, flop, flop, on the ground, like a window shade on a windy day.

We learned to love pain. Most NFL teams can't keep their guys on the field once they get dinged. In Houston, they laughed at you if you weren't out there. If a guy was truly injured, we didn't want him to come back before it was safe. I've never asked a trainer if we could play a guy with a bad injury. But what makes me mad is when a guy goes on injured reserve and he's happy to be there. Nobody likes a guy who just cashes his paychecks while the other guys play.

My first few years in Houston, I'd ask a trainer about a player's rehabilitation, and I'd get the same story every time. "He just needs rest," they'd say. "Time will do it."

We changed that thinking, and that was a big plus to our football team. In the NFL, we don't *have* time. We're hanging at the end of a short rope, and it's unraveling. If an injury's not serious, get the man back on the field. Our players in Houston were very cruel to injured players, unless, of course, they were seriously injured. They would call them "Lassie." The dog on the TV show used to always come home limping and whining. So whenever a player started complaining about an injury, the whole team would whine and whistle at him. They left one guy a bag of dog food in his locker. Lassies got very little respect on that football team. And, of course, they could spot a Lassie on another team in a heartbeat. If the Oilers thought you were a Lassie, you were in for a long day.

One day we woke up and the Houston Oilers were a real football team again. We had done most everything we had set out to accomplish. We were playing more bump-and-run than any team in football. We were blitzing more than any team in the NFL. We could throw deep whenever we wanted. We were gang tackling. We were standing up for ourselves and fighting when necessary.

The fans started coming back to the Astrodome, which linebacker Robert Lyles had affectionately named "The House of Pain." That's when I knew our message had sunk in with the players. The local press still didn't want anything to do with us, but we were all over the national media. Soon there were "House of Pain" hats, T-shirts, logos, you name it. And with the crowd behind us, we were unbeatable in the House of Pain. The players were proud of their reputation. We lost one home game all season.

There was something special about playing in the Astrodome back then. The turf was the oldest turf in the league, and it had seams so wide that small guys, like Ernie Givens, would fall in and be lost for days. We knew where all the bad seams were, of course, but other teams didn't. I've seen guys start running back kickoffs and just trip and fall down without being hit. And it was harder than concrete. We called the field "the green driveway."

It was horrible, but I believe when somebody throws you two lemons, you make lemonade. We turned it into a positive. We loved watching other teams come in and make ugly faces as they walked around the field, staring at the huge holes, the seams, the rips, the poor footing. It was all part of our fair advantage.

We also heard reports in recent years that there were huge cockroaches in the visitors' locker room. Raiders tight end Todd Christensen said that the roaches "are so big in there you could ride them out to the bus. They're bigger than rats." Well, we never saw any roaches in *our* locker room, so we never checked out the other locker room.

Ah, the luxuries of home.

6

Two Tickets to Paradise

Football is very, very serious in my family. But to get through the long grind, you have to find a way to make life a little lighter between contests. For twenty-seven years, I—and everybody close to me—have lived one weekend at a time, one war after another. Football at any level is violent, it's pressure, it's stress. The National Football League magnifies all those things about three times.

Humor is my way out. When I took the job as head coach of the Houston Oilers on January 20, 1986, everybody was pretty uptight. Everyone in the entire front office had their jaws set, they were afraid to smile. But the day I took the job, I told everybody there that on Sundays we were going to play reckless, smash-mouth football, and afterward we were going to have fun and relax. And I'll do the same in Atlanta. I'll tell the Falcons on their first day of camp that they're going to play harder than ever and laugh harder than ever.

The NFL has gone full circle. For a while, the league

was full of IBM coaches who took themselves too seriously. And the teams who didn't have an IBM executive went looking for one. They wanted a two-piece suit, wingtip shoes, maybe a vest, and a whole lot of hair spray. So for a while, that was all you saw. The sidelines looked like modeling studios. Perfect suits, perfect knots in their ties, perfect haircuts.

But now they've given up on the sleek, rubber-stamp coaches, and, thank God, they're hiring *football* people again. Guys just a little overweight, their shirttails hanging out in the back, and maybe just a little short. You won't find a necktie in that group. In fact, I get a thrill every time an ex-defensive coordinator gets a head coaching job. You won't find a defensive coordinator who looks like a male model. At least, nobody's ever accused me of that.

But that's where I fit in, or don't fit in, depending on how you look at it. Our teams don't do everything like everybody else. And we don't want to. And when the IBM clones and male models around the league see us having a good time, they don't like it. But humor is a drug, and we believe in large doses. So over the course of the past few years, we've had a little fun with all the stuffed shirts around the league—for me, leaving tickets and playing around is just a great way to take the pressure off yourself and the team on the road. But some coaches get upset with me. Well, I think what happens is that there are only twenty-eight of these jobs, and some guys, when they get one, start taking themselves too seriously. I've learned something in life, though. The jobs are going to go on whether you're there or not, so you might as well enjoy them. You might as well just go out and have fun.

I'll be honest. When I left two tickets at the will-call window for Elvis Presley, I never anticipated the reaction it created. The phone calls, cards and letters from all over the world absolutely shocked me. To this day, half of my daily stack of mail concerns Elvis Presley. I'm repeatedly asked, "Why did you do it?" People don't want to believe that it was simply a fun way to break up a road trip in the middle of a long, hot training camp.

But then I started getting more letters. And more phone calls. From the nuttiest people. Would you believe James Dean? Marilyn Monroe? That's when I stated feeling guilty. Who was I to invite Elvis Presley to a game and not invite James Dean? Was I implying that Elvis was more important than the great James Dean? Of course not. So I did the right thing.

When we played in Indianapolis, we left tickets for James Dean, a native of nearby Fairmount, Indiana. As I said, he's one of my all-time favorites. I even named my '50 Mercury after him, the "James Dean Special." During that trip to Indianapolis, we got a chance to tour James Dean's grave site, and the mayor of Fairmount made us special guests that afternoon. It was really touching. Like Elvis, James Dean lived right on the edge. I've got the last photograph ever taken of James Dean, right after he filled his Spider up with gas and was headed out of the gas station. Six miles down the road, he was killed in a tragic accident.

Ever since I left him tickets, I feel closer to James Dean every day. His family has sent me photographs. His former classmates have sent me pictures. I've got his senior track photo, his high school graduation photo, his sophomore class photo. Most people don't even know he wore glasses his senior year in high school. Glasses! Can you believe it? Every time I put the James Dean Special in a car show, we display all the memorabilia I've collected. We were showing the car once in Houston, when an old man walked up with a gold, antiqued etching of James Dean, handed it to me and turned to walk away.

"Wait a minute," I said. "Why are you giving this to me?"

"I've had that a long, long time," the old guy said. "And I just figure you can do more with it than I can."

When we went to New York to play the Jets, I left tickets for the Phantom of the Opera. This started a unique turn of events. Michael Crawford, who was the original phantom on Broadway, in turn sent *me* tickets for the play in New York. So when I got back to Houston, we auctioned them off for $3,400 and donated the money to the Ronald McDonald House in Houston.

The Philadelphia connection is a bit more confusing. I knew that both W. C. Fields and Ed McMahon were from Philly and figured it would be nice to leave them each a ticket. But the more I thought about it, the more confusing it got. Have you ever seen W. C. Fields and Ed McMahon in the same place? Could it be that they're the *same* guy? So I left one. For both of them.

Then there's Pittsburgh. What a great place. They can't

even get my name right in Pittsburgh. Every time we used to play there, the announcer said, " . . . and the Houston Oilers, coached by Gary Grandview." I got chills down my spine every time he said that. Usually when we play on the road, it's hard to keep our players from being too distracted. Like when we play in San Diego, they're more concerned about going to the San Diego Zoo than they are about team meetings. Pittsburgh, however, doesn't quite have those distractions. I've never heard of anybody who wanted to take some vacation time and check out the Pittsburgh Zoo.

The people in Pittsburgh really love each other. They have to, because what else could keep them there? Once when I was with Houston and we played in Pittsburgh, I left tickets for Charles Wilkenhauser, the director of the Pittsburgh Zoo.

Somebody asked me, "Why would you leave tickets for a guy who is alive, when all your other guests were allegedly dead?"

Well, I assumed Wilkenhauser was bored to death, so that was close enough. I left him two passes so he could come to our game and see some real animals.

I'm told Pittsburgh has become a better place to live since then. I understand they might even start a bus tour of the city, sort of like they have in Beverly Hills. The driver will take you by some boring house and say, "This is where Chuck Noll lives." Ain't that special? I predict tourists will just flock to this special attraction.

Cincinnati is unique, too. We left passes for Loni Anderson, who made Cincinnati famous for two reasons when she starred on the "WKRP" television show. At least, everybody watched that show for *two* reasons. We started to leave her two tickets for those obvious reasons, but then we decided to leave her just one. I was afraid she might misunderstand and invite her husband Burt Reynolds, who can't go out the door without his toupee. Think about it: Nobody in America knows what Burt Reynolds looks like bald except for Loni Anderson. That's a scary thought. Without the toupee, Burt could probably double as the Phantom of the Opera.

Seattle has the worst sense of humor. We left tickets for D. B. Cooper, who a lot of young kids probably didn't remember. D. B. Cooper robbed a bank in the great Northwest, then parachuted out of an airplane over a densely wooded area while the police were hot on his trail. That's a spooky deal, because they never found his body, they never found the money, they never found anything. When the Federal Bureau of Investigation found out I'd left him tickets, they panicked. It's a real touchy subject with them. I found out later that the FBI has spent more money trying to find him than what he originally stole. That's the government for you. But because he is still at large, they thought maybe, just maybe, ol' D.B. might not be able to resist a chance to see a football game for free. And I can't say I blame them for their reasoning.

So the FBI had to stake out the ticket booth to see if he would show up. I didn't do it on purpose, but because of me, the FBI ended up spending still *more* money on

D. B. Cooper. He didn't show up at will call, but I did
hear that the two FBI agents enjoyed the game.

Once, when I was coaching in Houston, we went up
to play the Dallas Cowboys, and Houston fans and Dallas
fans agreed on something, probably for the first time in
their lives. I got fan mail from Dallas and Houston all
week prior to the game, begging me to leave tickets for
Buddy Holly, the great rock 'n' roll singer. He was a
Texas boy, I believe from Lubbock, and he sure knew
how to sing. So I left him a couple of tickets to watch
us beat the Cowboys. Now I get mail from him, too, but
not too often. Next time we talk, however, I'm going to
ask Buddy to send me his glasses, because we've got
about a dozen referees in the league who need to use
them. Unfortunately, they probably won't be strong
enough.

Cleveland is always a unique trip. I was there with the
Oilers twice during 1987 and 1988. Actually, playing
in dilapidated Cleveland Stadium really pulls our team
together, it unifies us. It's not so much the game, but
when you have fifty-five guys and only two shower heads
in the locker room, it really brings out a sense of camara-
derie that we just didn't feel in most other NFL cities.
On our last trip to Cleveland, I took my own nail and
hammer so I'd have a place to hang my shirt.

What really excited the Oilers, though, was the chance
to play on painted dirt, which Cleveland officials mistak-
enly refer to as a playing surface. That's what it is—
painted dirt. When it snows, they even paint the snow

green. Incredible. The first time I left tickets in Cleveland, I left them for three of my former high school coaches. The second time, however, I left them for Elliott Ness, the great crime fighter who arrested Al Capone for income tax evasion.

Going to Buffalo is always fun because I used to coach there. The year before I hired on in Houston as the defensive coordinator, I spent a year in Buffalo as an assistant coach. At the time, I had two job offers; one in California and one in Buffalo. I told my wife, Brenda, we were going to Buffalo. She immediately checked with her lawyers about an insanity charge. I got her a snow shovel for Christmas and had her name engraved on it. She cried when we went to Buffalo, but she cried when we left, too.

Buffalo turned out to be a great experience. In Orchard Park, where the Bills' stadium is, you get pre-World War II prices on houses. We got a great deal. You wouldn't believe how cheap it is in Buffalo to take your family to dinner. You could walk to the grocery store and the post office. Everybody owned a sled. It was like one big Norman Rockwell painting.

When I left tickets in Buffalo, I couldn't make up my mind who deserved them the most. I thought about Jay Silverheels, the actor who played Tonto in "The Lone Ranger." He was born in Buffalo. My second choice was Dabney Coleman, for his television show "Buffalo Bill." My third choice was Paul Maguire's liver, which died years ago. Paul, who played for the Bills and is now an NBC analyst, still lives in Buffalo.

I finally decided on Dabney Coleman. "Buffalo Bill" was a great show. Dabney Coleman represented everybody who's ever been in the media—rude, crude and stupid. But that's another chapter.

7

A Wrestler, The President and a Dead Guy

The 1987 season got off to an auspicious start. Houston beat the Los Angeles Rams at home, then went to Buffalo and got beat, 34–30. We were 1–1, and in first place in the AFC Central Division. Then, on the flight home from Buffalo, the players informed us they would not be back, that the NFL Players Association was going on strike.

The union's biggest issue was free agency, which the owners were never going to give up. But I'm not into issues. I'm a football coach. I get paid to coach whoever shows up for work. On the airplane that night, I told our players to do whatever they had to do, but do it as a team. More than ever, stick together. Then I went back up front with the rest of Houston's coaches.

The players had gone on a fifty-seven-day strike in 1982, when I was with the Atlanta Falcons. For nearly two months of the season, there was no football. I figured we were in for another layoff. The 1982 season had been a nightmare. Every week the coaching staff prepared for that week's opponent, drew up a game plan and went through the motions, just in case the players returned. *Not again,* I thought to myself.

But then Ladd Herzeg, Houston's general manager at the time, informed the coaching staff that the league office had decided to continue playing. "You better get some players," he told us, "because it looks like we're playing again in two weeks."

Oh boy. I could tell immediately that this was going to be a humdinger. I had coached replacement players before. When I was in Detroit, the players went on strike during the preseason for about six weeks. We had a center that we got out of a bar somewhere, where he had been singing Peter, Paul and Mary songs. We lined up against the Raiders, and none of their players had walked out. So we put a folksinger across from Bubba Smith. Our quarterback was so scared he wouldn't take the snap. But that strike had ended before the regular season. This time, the games would count.

So right there on the plane, I huddled with my other coaches, and we started talking about players. June Jones had spent a few years coaching in the defunct United States Football League, so he started naming off guys that might help us. We started scribbling names down on napkins, magazines, whatever we could get our hands on.

Before we got off the plane, I told the players what was going on. They got a big chuckle out of it. I don't honestly think they ever believed we would play with replacement players. And quite frankly, I couldn't imagine it either. But we told our real players that when the strike was over, they'd still be in first place. If the games were going to count, our staff was going to find a way to win.

The second we landed in Houston, our coaching staff went back to work. We began a massive manhunt for players. We made phone call after phone call. I felt like a college recruiter again. I'd call a college coach and ask, "Who did you have last year that wasn't *too* bad? Can he be here by tomorrow?"

Our coaching staff worked twenty-four hours straight and sent plane tickets out all over the country. Then we waited for that first day of practice. Not knowing what to expect, I put on my coaching shorts and T-shirt and headed out to the practice field. Now, I'd been coaching in the NFL for fifteen years. I'd seen some pretty bad players in a few training camps. But nothing could have prepared me for this.

The first day, we had seventeen players. Actually, we had seventeen people. *Players* would be stretching it. Our real players were lined up outside the fence surrounding the practice field yelling and throwing eggs.

"Hey," a heckler shouted at a former Michigan player. "You're not a Wolverine, you're a Listerine!"

We started out by trying to put a roster together. One guy, Sam Moore, said he had been a receiver at Texas El Paso. Another guy claimed to be Bubba Bean, who had played at Texas A & M and had been in Atlanta when I was there. Five other guys had never played football before, but said they were quick learners.

Practice began. In the meantime, Mike Holovak started

making phone calls to confirm everybody's story. When he talked to a coach at Texas El Paso, he was shocked. "The guy you say you have," the coach said, "supposedly died in a car wreck about three years ago. He's dead."

When Mike told me that, I wasn't too surprised. The guy certainly played like he was dead. And I wasn't too sure about Bubba Bean, either. The more I looked at "Bubba Bean," the more he looked old enough to be Bubba's father. But when you only have seventeen guys, you don't tell anybody to leave. Then our two quarterbacks decided they couldn't take the heckling and split. So an hour into the first practice, I've got five guys who never played, one is dead and two just quit.

"Gentlemen," I said to my coaches, "it's going to be a long day."

Things got a little better. At least more bodies started coming through the doors, which gave us more to work with. We had quite an assortment. Four of our players were high school coaches. Another guy was so fat he would've turned queer for a chocolate sundae. We took linebacker Eugene Seale off a jackhammer in Beaumont, Texas, where he'd been earning $4 an hour. Eugene hadn't played in two years, and his cleats hurt his feet so bad he practiced in his socks. Eric Cobble, a running back, was an instructor at the Texas State School for the Blind.

At safety we had Craig Birdsong, a professional wrestler. At guard was Doug Kellermeyer, an opera singer. Offensive lineman Charles Agee and linebacker Scott Stoughton were death row prison guards with the Texas

Department of Corrections. Charles told me that the biggest change for him was that he finally could say, "See you guys tomorrow." On his old job, he was never sure.

Another running back named Andrew Jackson, who called himself "The President," had been unloading trucks for $1,500 a month. Our other wide receiver, Matt Conerly, who had played at New Mexico State, was a black belt in karate. He actually went to the fence and *taunted* the striking players.

"I'll take any of you one on one," he said.

The fence paid for itself that day.

The NFL started calling to tell us that half our players either *weren't* players or weren't who they claimed to be. That really built our confidence. But we kept at it, morning, afternoon and night. We had all the replacement players in a nearby hotel and brought them to practice every day in a big Greyhound bus. We practiced twice a day and worked on special teams at night under the lights of that Greyhound. We even put them through the same weight and conditioning program as the regulars, which nearly killed half of them.

After about a week, we had our first live scrimmage.

"OK, guys," I said. "This is your chance to go live, 100 miles per hour, full contact."

The whistle blew, and that was the last sound we heard all day. No crack of helmets. No pads popping. I'd seen better powder-puff games. These guys didn't hit; heck, they didn't even grab. There was a lot of pushing and shoving. We heard somebody singing in the offensive line. Eugene was sliding around in his socks. The wrestler was body-slamming running backs. The karate kid was kicking people.

Later that night, we took a look at the film. It was hilarious. Our coaches were rolling on the floor, kicking their feet in the air and laughing hysterically until tears rolled down their cheeks.

But I realized after about nine days that not a single coach, including me, had offered a single compliment to these guys. So I told the coaches to *find* something positive, get it in the players' minds that they were a decent football team. From that day on, we never said another negative word.

In the next team meeting, we told the players that we had to get that Oiler mentality, that Oiler temperament. "You have to start smacking people," I said. "We've got to hit to the whistle."

One of the players stood up. "We may be scabs," he said, "but for however long this thing lasts, let's be the *best* scabs in the NFL."

They ran out the door with a roar. I felt like I was back at Georgia Tech. These guys had incredible enthusiasm.

Finally the impossible became the inevitable. Our team boarded a plane for Denver, where we would meet the replacement Broncos. That's when the surprises really started. At halftime, we were up by 30 points. When it was over, we'd won, 40–10. It was a very unusual experience—we were trying not to run up the score. The offense generated 414 yards. Eugene Seale, wearing shoes for the first time in two weeks, returned an interception 73 yards for a touchdown. Quarterback Brent

Pease completed fifteen of twenty-five passes for 260 yards and a touchdown. The President rushed for 102 yards. It was the most amazing thing I'd ever seen. Pease even picked up a blitz and threw a touchdown to a guy that a week earlier couldn't have run down to the 7-Eleven.

In the first half, we lined up in the shotgun and had the center direct-snap the ball to the running back, who lined up next to the quarterback. The first time we ran it, it went for a touchdown. The referee came over to me afterward.

"We think that play is illegal," he said. "The quarterback can't hold his hands out unless he's going to get the snap."

I gave the ref a confused look. "Mr. Ref," I said, looking perfectly innocent, "our center's only been snapping a football for about three days. We have no idea *where* it's going."

"I apologize," he said. The touchdown stood.

What surprised me after the game was the reaction of the Houston media, which is typically pretty negative. They seemed to enjoy watching the new Oilers. One columnist pointed out that it was the biggest Houston road victory in twelve years and only the fourth road win in the last forty-four tries. We gave out some fifty-eight game balls, to every player who made the trip, which cost us $2,668. But they were the happiest guys in the world.

The strike continued. So we headed to Cleveland with a 2–1 record and tied with the Browns and the Steelers for first place. We got into Cleveland late that Saturday afternoon. We bused down to "the mistake by the lake," good old Cleveland Stadium.

Cleveland, which is really a big union town, supported the players' strike. When we got to the stadium, we piled off the bus, but when we got to the gate, a security guard stopped us.

"You ain't coming in," he said. "Go practice somewhere else."

My wrestler, Craig Birdsong, got this weird look in his eyes.

"You want me to body-slam him, coach?" he asked.

Our two prison guards started getting anxious, like they wanted to give the guard the old cell-block treatment.

"I will use force," the guard said. "You're not coming in."

Our players all looked at me. I just smiled and turned my back. I heard a lot of yelling and banging, but I didn't actually *see* anything. All I know is the security guard just vanished.

We practiced, and we beat Cleveland, 15–10. During that game, we had a guy knock his shoulder out of the socket. We didn't even *have* a backup at that position.

"Tape me up," he said. "I'll go."

So we taped his arm to his chest, and he played the second half with one arm. He couldn't tackle, but he put his head down and butted the hell out of some people. Every week our staff was just amazed at the effort these guys gave.

The third week of replacement games brought the strike to a head. the striking players had decided to pursue their demands through the courts, which is probably the route they should have taken in the first place. But there was great debate about when the players would return to their jobs. The owners ordered the players to be back by Wednesday of that week, or they would not play or be paid for another week.

Meanwhile, the replacement players kept practicing. Wednesday came and went. But about 1 P.M. on Thursday, practice was interrupted by great commotion in the parking lot. The real Oilers had decided to return to their jobs; the strike was over. They all showed up, but security wouldn't let them in. The owners stuck by their threat: The replacement players would play a final week.

The owners agreed to allow the real players to practice, however. So on Friday, I took a double dose of Maalox and reported to work. It was really weird. We had the replacement players in the morning. In the afternoon, we had the real players. The coaches were almost giddy. We had real players again! Guys with speed and quickness and size. It was like Christmas.

But in spite of my excitement over the end of the strike, I couldn't help but appreciate our ragtag group of replacements. I'll never forget the feeling in that locker room when they dressed for our last game, a home game against New England.

"This is it," I told them. "We'll never be together again. We've come a long way, and most of the guys in this room will go different directions after today. But for what it's worth, we appreciate every guy in this room."

Listening to the comments around the room made me emotional.

"We went through some tough times," Andrew Jackson told his teammates, "but we overcame them and pulled together as a team. I'm gonna miss you guys."

"For three weeks, I was a Houston Oiler," said Eugene Seale, who had finally grown accustomed to cleats. "Not a scab, but a Houston Oiler. I'll always remember that."

When we lined up for the national anthem, there wasn't a dry eye on the sideline. But New England beat us, 21–7.

It was a tough day when we sent most of the strike players home. The night they all flew out, I was watching the news on television with Steve Watterson, our strength coach. There was a story about an airplane that had slid off the runway and was stuck in the mud for about three hours.

"I bet our fat boy was on that plane," I joked. "He had a few more sundaes in the airport, and they couldn't get him off the ground."

I found out the next day that he *was* on that plane.

Some stories had a happy ending. A half dozen of Houston's replacement players, including quarterback Brent Pease, center Billy Kidd and safety Domingo Bryant, spent time on the Oilers' regular roster during the next two seasons. Wide receiver Leonard Harris and safety Kenny Johnson are still there. And linebacker Eugene Seale not only made the team, but has become one of the best special teams players in the NFL.

Players, coaches, unions, fans—everybody had an opinion about the strike and the replacement players. But I know one thing: Without those two victories, Houston never would've made the playoffs that year. That was a critical stage in the development of the veterans they have today.

So call them scabs, replacements, scumbags or whatever. All I know is they were winners. And nobody can take that away from them.

8

My Hero, Chuck Noll

There is no love lost between coaches in the Central Division of the AFC. It's the only division in the NFL where the coaches don't get together in the off-season and talk football. Which is a darn good thing, because I can't imagine anything worse than spending a week with Chuck Noll.

To understand why Chuck and I don't get along, you have to back up a little. For many, many years, the Pittsburgh Steelers rolled through Houston like a bad storm. We never knew what hit us. They'd punch us in the mouth, and we'd wait for the flag and go back to the huddle. In the past, they had big bullies like Jack Lambert and "Mean" Joe Greene—you know, the famous "Steel Curtain" stuff. Frightening, isn't it? Of course, Noll's players never did anything wrong. I'm sure Lambert never hit a quarterback after the whistle, or hit a running back after he was out of bounds.

The truth is, the Steelers used to play like they were possessed. They were an intimidating, punishing football team. They played the game like it should be played. Before I went to Houston in 1984, Chuck Noll interviewed me. It was pretty amazing. We agreed on everything: aggressiveness, play-to-the-whistle, all that stuff. For whatever reasons, he didn't hire me. And every day of my life I breathe a little prayer of thanks for that.

But his attitude changed drastically when we started playing aggressive football in Houston. Actually, his attitude changed when we started beating him. Going into the 1987 season, the Steelers had beaten us twenty-six times, more than any other team in the NFL. In 1985, I can remember him saying, "You're doing a great coaching job. I hope they keep you forever." But that changed on November 16, 1987, when we played the Steelers at Three Rivers Stadium in Pittsburgh.

This game came at a time when the Oilers were looking for an identity. With the exception of wide receiver Louis Lipps and center Mike Webster, Noll had lost most of his great players to retirement. And his best quarterback, Bubby Brister, was sitting on the bench behind a used-up landmark named Mark Malone.

The Oilers understood what it meant to play Pittsburgh. They knew the Steelers had made doormats out of Houston in the late seventies and early eighties. In 1987, the Oilers were just starting to be contenders again in the Central Division. We wanted to sweep Pittsburgh for the first time, not just because we didn't like them, but because we needed the victories to get in the playoffs.

I didn't give any pregame speeches. Pregame speeches

are for boola-boola college boys. There was no big locker room pep talk. Talk has never won a football game in the NFL. You can't talk an attitude, you have to *have* an attitude. Anything a coach says only lasts until you get punched in the mouth on the first play. Then you're on your own.

Each player has a different starter button, and you just try to push as many of them as you can. Every player gets ready for a big game in a different way. Some guys beat their heads against the wall. Some read comic books. We simply tell our players, "Do whatever it takes to get yourself ready to play. But when you run down that tunnel and step out on that turf, you better be ready."

We lined up in the tunnel. Guys were bouncing on their toes, smacking their fists and breathing fire. You should have seen the looks in their eyes. It looked like somebody had given forty-five guys at a mental institution a weekend pass. Finally the time came to take the field. The boos were deafening.

"Ladies and gentlemen," the announcer roared, "let's welcome Gary Grandview and the rest of the Houston Oilers."

The chills shot up and down my spine as we poured out of the tunnel. Every tackle we made in that game sounded like a car wreck. Pads were popping, helmets were cracking. Pittsburgh loves to run trap plays, and we were ready. They ran Ernest Jackson off right tackle. *Whap.* John Grimsley met him in the hole and stood him up straight. Jackson vanished under a pile of white jerseys.

Pittsburgh ran Frank Pollard off left tackle. *Crack.* Nose tackle Richard Byrd picked him up, drove him back, and hammered him to the turf, followed by ten more white helmets. On the sidelines, I was smiling. We had preached toughness. We had drafted toughness. And it was finally becoming reality on the field. You can't camouflage toughness. Houston receivers laugh at guys who *won't* go over the middle. And their center, Jay Pennison, is completely nuts, he's tougher than a $2 steak. What made me proud back then was our level of confidence. Nobody was cheap-shotting anybody. Nobody was hitting late. We were just being downright nasty and physical, and doing it with an air of confidence that I'd never seen in this team before.

Pittsburgh wasn't happy. They started getting angry. Five years earlier, if the Pittsburgh players had started roughing us up, our guys would've gone into a shell. Not anymore. Pittsburgh threw a few punches. Surprise! We punched them back. That really confused them.

It was still early in the game when the first of several "incidents" involving their running backs took place. We don't respect people who play on the edges, who run out of bounds. Or hit the pile and stop moving and wait on the whistle. Houston's backs, guys like Allen Pinkett, Mike Rozier and Alonzo Highsmith, *never* ran out of bounds. In 1988, Rozier had a 1,000-yard season, but most importantly, 448 of those yards came *after* the first tackler arrived. Houston may be the only team in the NFL to chart yardage after the initial hit.

Not so with Ernest Jackson. He'd run it up in there,

get stopped and wait for the whistle. Or run wide and end up in a footrace to the sidelines, with one of our defensive backs in hot pursuit. It was late in the first quarter, and Jackson, who was the NFL's leading rusher at the time, had managed just 1 yard on four carries. He took a swing pass in the flat and turned upfield.

Linebacker Robert Lyles roared out of nowhere and popped Jackson, who was stunned but didn't fall down. No whistle. Jackson stumbled forward. Instantly, there was a collision, like a baseball bat hitting a side of beef. Two more Oilers, Al Smith and Charles Martin, finished him off with a splat. Nothing cheap. Nothing dirty. Just a good splat. No flags.

Jackson didn't get up. He left the game with a bruised back. On the Steelers' sideline, Noll was screaming at the side judge that it was a late hit. We continued to play our brand of football for the next three quarters, and the Steelers wanted no part of it. We won, 23–3.

After the game, Noll went crazy. He accused us of spearing. He said we hit late all day and that we used our helmets "with the intention of ending people's careers."

"We're not making a big deal out of it," Noll told reporters after the game. "Except we did lose our running back who has been very productive for us. We will handle it ourselves if the league office doesn't."

Noll added that not only did the Oilers cheap-shot players, but also that I taught them to do it. "They are encouraged to do it, no doubt about it," Noll said. "They have a propensity for that."

That last quote impressed me, because I'd never heard

a football coach use a big word like *propensity*. But that was nothing. Later in the week, he told the *Houston Chronicle* that the Oilers "have a *proclivity* for spearing." When the press asked me to respond, I refused to comment. After that display of vocabulary, what could I possibly say?

December 21, 1987, finally rolled around. Every day since the first game, Chuck had hyped this game. "If the league doesn't do something about it, we may go spearing ourselves," Noll promised. Our players couldn't wait. "I was fired up for this game," said our nose tackle, Doug Smith. "Why? Because they showed up. That's all I needed." Lineman Richard Byrd was pumped up, too. "We heard all week that Pittsburgh was going to come in here and kick our butts, legally or illegally. We were ready."

Pittsburgh, welcome to the House of Pain.

Our goal was to put them away early. From the very beginning, we set the tempo. Jeff Donaldson intercepted two passes. Our quarterback hit two bombs to Drew Hill, one for 52 yards and one for 30 yards. John Grimsley had seventeen tackles.

The most satisfying part of the game was that we wore them out physically. Of course, they protested again. With eleven minutes and forty seconds remaining in the third quarter, Pittsburgh ran Frank Pollard inside on another trap play. Doug Smith stuffed him, and Pollard quit moving, waiting on a whistle. About six or seven of our guys, including lineman Richard Byrd, dove into the fray, driving Pollard about 10 yards behind the line of scrimmage. Finally a whistle blew.

Pollard blew at the same time. He threw the ball at Dickie Byrd and took a swing. Big mistake. What was I supposed to do? Tell our guys to take a punch in the mouth, walk away from it like a wimp and become a radio or TV journalist? We don't punch first. But we don't walk away, either. So Dickie flew all over Pollard, followed by Doug Smith.

"I don't know exactly what happened," Smith told Jim Carley of the *Houston Post*. "But [Pollard] threw the ball, and it just went from there. We knew it was going to be an emotional game. Nobody was disappointed."

Especially the fans. While Smith and Byrd wrestled Pollard to the ground, a free-for-all broke out between the 10- and 40-yard line on our end of the field. Fists were flying. Flags were flying. Whistles were blowing.

When things got settled down, they kicked out Dickie Byrd, Doug Smith and Frank Pollard. I still don't understand how their guy starts a fight, their whole team gets involved, and we lose two and they lose one. Incredible. But the beauty of the whole scene was that they lost their composure. We didn't lose ours. The fight, which *they* instigated, gave *us* the momentum. We won, 24–16.

When the gun sounded, I turned to run to our locker room. I noticed Chuck running across the field toward me. I thought he was going to congratulate me on our first sweep of Pittsburgh in team history. So I smiled and extended my hand. He took it, shook it and kept shaking. His face got all red. I thought he was becoming infatuated with my hand.

"Your f . . . . . . guys coming over, jumping on people like that, are going to get your ass in trouble," Chuck roared, pointing his finger at my chest. "Just know that."

I turned to walk away, but Noll wouldn't let go.

"I'm serious," he yelled.

What a guy.

After the game, Chuck got back on his soapbox. First he filed a complaint with the NFL's competition committee, his second of the year against us. Then he lashed out at me. He accused me of "absolute cheap-shotting. [Glanville's] teams have led the league in personal fouls everywhere he's been." Now that was a total lie. When I was an assistant at Buffalo, we didn't lead the league in *anything*.

It was childish. Here's a guy who coached Jack Lambert, Mean Joe Greene, L. C. Greenwood, and he's telling me *my* guys are too violent? The great thing about football is that contact is part of the game. It's not like hockey, where you give sticks to a bunch of ornery guys and beg them not to kill each other. Chuck's biggest problem wasn't the hitting. He just couldn't believe Houston had beaten him twice. I'm sure it made him want to slit his wrists.

I never complain about a game. I don't make excuses. But I had to respond to Chuck's accusations. So we had our team film crew put together a videotape for us that showed at least seven plays in which a Houston player was the recipient of a cheap hit from a Pittsburgh player. We're not lily-white, but it goes both ways.

The Houston reporters were licking their lips at my press conference the day after the game. Here I was, a young head coach in the league, getting ripped by a living legend. "This is for your knowledge, which I realize is hard to add to," I told the press. "We put this tape together to let you decide what's dangerous. I should be the guy upset and making threats about how the game was played."

I made it clear that I was not complaining. The Steelers play physical, hard-nosed football. I'll never cry about that. But I wasn't going to apologize for our gang-tackling, swarming and hitting, either. We take pride in getting one more helmet on the football.

The videotape told no lies. Our quarterback was speared. Mike Rozier was hit late. Offensive lineman Bruce Matthews was punched on the chin, which later required three stitches. Mike Munchak was shoved in the face. We should have showed the press the entire game.

Our guys handled the situation with class. In that infamous game, only one team was called for spearing, and it wasn't us. But that game established Houston's identity. Thanks to Chuck Noll, the Oilers now had a reputation around the NFL as a team that wouldn't quit, wouldn't back down, wouldn't walk away from a fight. Chuck had given Houston the identity it had been looking for.

Two days after the game, I paid $9.70 to send Chuck a letter through Federal Express, telling him to look at

the game film before he made any more unfounded accusations. He claims he never got the letter. I still have
the receipt. Maybe the Federal Express man couldn't find
Pittsburgh on the map, or maybe he didn't know who
Chuck Noll was. I don't know.

But the season ended, and I thought the feud was over.
I was wrong. In March, the NFL brings all the head
coaches together for league meetings. These big meetings
are like fish—after three days, they stink. Put twenty-
eight coaches in the same room and it won't take long
before everybody's bored or arguing. Make that twenty-
seven—Buddy Ryan never shows up, which might make
him the smartest coach in football.

Noll cornered a few reporters at the 1988 league meetings and started on us again. His comments made
national news and headlines in Pittsburgh and Houston.

"The Oilers will pay for their aggressiveness," he said.
"They will have a lot of people come back after them the
same way. All this stuff does is make for a fight—it'll be
like a hockey game. I think they have the philosophy
that the officials are going to get tired of throwing a flag
on every play. But I don't think the game should be
played like this—it's physical enough without Glanville
trying to end people's careers."

Noll grabbed every reporter he could find to explain
"special tackling tactics" that our team used against the
Steelers. He told Bill Utterback of the *Pittsburgh Press*
that we teach our defense "to hold a ballcarrier erect
while other players dive at the ballcarrier's knees." Then

he told Ed Bouchette of the *Pittsburgh Post-Gazette* that the Oilers "hold people up and go for their ribs."

If we can't hit you in the legs or in the chest, Chuck, where *do* we tackle you? But Noll wasn't finished. Someone asked him to compare the "new" Houston Oilers to the old Oakland Raiders of the 1970s, who Noll once blasted in federal court for condoning a "criminal element" for "intentionally hurting other players."

"Oh, the Raiders just played good, hard football," he said. "The Raiders had a problem with individuals. With Houston, it's the entire team."

Can't anybody lose a game in this league without crying? I thought. *I'll promise you this: We may win big or lose big, but we don't dodge anybody and we don't make excuses when we lose. We never have, and we never will.* In 1988, we set a goal for the players: We challenged them to break one hundred face masks. Our equipment manager had seventy-five face masks in stock when the season started. By week twelve, we had broken every one of them.

Since 1987, the Oilers have won five out of seven games with Pittsburgh. When the Oilers played up there in 1989 in a driving snowstorm, the fans cheered the snow. That was the first time I'd ever heard a crowd cheer the weather. The harder it snowed, the louder they yelled. It sounded like 80,000 people, but they had more than 20,000 no-shows.

The Oilers have come a long way in recent years. But the Steelers put them on the map. Chuck had a lot to do with how other people perceived them. They really should thank him, but as for me personally, it kills me to give him credit for anything. Ever since then, I've never shaken his hand, either.

He got me once, but he won't get me twice.

9

Motorcycles, Rabbits and Jerry Jeff

I really can't remember how or when I started being so superstitious, but the fact is, I believe in doing whatever it takes to win a football game. If it means wearing the same socks, the same shirt, the same underwear, well then, do it.

Every time you win a game, the very next week you have to do everything *exactly* like you did it the week before. But if you lose, then you change everything. You don't do anything the same way—you have to break the pattern and get on a new streak. Understand, this is all very scientific, very space age.

When I was an assistant coach, in my early days with the Atlanta Falcons, I always wore my cowboy hat on road games. The players noticed that when I didn't wear a cowboy hat on a road trip, we got beat. We also started listening to Willie Nelson's "On the Road Again" at the start of every trip. We'd crank it up and sing as loud as we could. At one time, Atlanta had one of the worst road records in the league. But look this up—the year I started wearing my cowboy hat and the team started playing Willie Nelson, we ended up with the best road record in the NFL. It's amazing what a hat and a song can do for a team. Imagine the fear other teams must have felt when they saw me step off the plane wearing my lucky hat and humming Willie Nelson.

"Uh-oh, he's wearing the hat!"

Of course, my motorcycle won a few games for us in Atlanta, too. Every Friday I'd ride my motorcycle to work as fast it would go. One day it hit me: Every time I rode the motorcycle on Friday, we won. When I didn't—you guessed it—we lost. Once after we got beat, Ted Plumb, another assistant coach, asked me what happened.

"I forgot to ride my motorcycle," I told him. It was so embarrassing.

"Maybe if I ride with you this week we'll be twice as lucky," Ted said.

So that Friday, Ted and I jumped on and we took off for the Falcons training facility with a roar. About ten minutes into the trip, I noticed Ted had his fingers dug into my rib cage. I checked the rearview mirrors, and his eyes were bugging out, his tongue was flapping in the wind and tears were streaming off his face like rain.

"How . . . fast . . . are . . . we . . . going?" he yelled.

"I don't know," I screamed back, "but we never go less than a hundred!"

When we got to the facility, he ran full-speed down to the basement, jumped in a hot tub and stayed there all morning. As it turned out, he was bad luck, anyhow. We lost that week. Which was a damn good thing for Ted; otherwise he would've had to ride with me the next week.

Working with Doug Shively, who has been with me for what feels like an eternity, is one of the biggest reasons I'm so superstitious. He's the final authority on what works or doesn't work. "If it worked once, it'll work again—you just have to believe," Shive says. I've been believing since Detroit, where I first got into the routine of singing "Sunday Morning Sidewalk," by Kris Kristofferson, every Sunday on my way to the game. I sang my butt off, but we didn't win a whole lot of games. I blamed my voice, not the song. My singing has emptied a church or two in my time.

When Shive and I attend church before a game, we always sit in the exact same seats that we sat in the last time. If we lose, we consider changing churches. Once we showed up for church and an entire family was sitting where we'd been sitting the week before. My heart sank— I was undefeated in this church at the time. We sat behind them. We lost. When something gets disrupted, even in church, it's really scary.

Like another time Shive and I attended early church the morning before a critical game. The ushers came around with the offering plates. The week before, I'd put a big check in the offering and we won big. So I reached down to write another check. Then I realized I had forgotten my checkbook.

"Shive," I whispered, "is it bad luck that I forgot my checkbook?"

Shive gulped and his eyes widened.

"I'm afraid so," he whispered back.

"Will it be worse luck if I go home and get it?"

Shive thought for a moment.

"I think maybe if we put in a bunch of cash, we could overcome the bad luck of not having the check," he answered.

Next thing you know, two grown men are shaking themselves down for cash in the middle of a church service. Women snickered and children laughed as Shive and I emptied our pockets, front and back, wallets, jacket pockets—everything—and dumped every bit of cash into the plate.

"That was close," Shive said, sighing.

Road trips are packed with superstitions, from start to finish. Just ask Floyd Reese, another former Houston assistant who has worked with me forever. During the 1988 season in Houston, we'd set out on our first road trip of the preseason when I noticed that Floyd, who's from California, had on khaki pants and the ugliest flowery summer shirt you've ever seen.

"Floyd, that outfit's either gonna get us killed or cause the other team to lose," I told him.

We won. When we got back on the plane, I made an announcement.

"For the rest of the year, Floyd, those are your lucky road clothes," I said.

Floyd laughed. But that was in August. You should've seen poor Floyd in December when we went to play Cleveland. Snow was coming down in sheets when we stepped off the plane. We were all bundled up in scarves, thick jackets, thermal underwear, anything we could get our hands on. Then Floyd stepped off in a short-sleeved, flower-print Hawaiian shirt. Now that's dedication to the cause.

Floyd also used to pick me up before games and take me to the team's facility, where we board the team bus for the airport. But that started getting us beat. Now I taxi Floyd. If I don't pick up Floyd, we don't have a chance of winning. I hate to say this, but another bad omen in Houston was my wife, Brenda. We never won a road game when she went with us. Whenever Floyd and I would pull into the facility, all the players in the bus would be craning their necks and straining their eyes to see if Brenda was in the car with us. One time we whipped into the parking lot, and Brenda hopped out.

I heard a huge, simultaneous sigh come from inside the bus. "Honey," I said, "I love you. But if we ever make the Super Bowl, the coaches have offered to pay for you to go to Hawaii that week. Nothing personal, just business."

Once on board the team bus, Floyd always sat behind the driver. I always sat in the very back of the bus, next to the commode. One time the driver handed me a plunger.

"We've had some trouble back here. Do me a favor. If anything goes wrong"—he pointed to the plunger—"just fix it."

I assured him that nobody could handle crap like an NFL head coach. "I do this for a living," I said.

Once we get to the plane, it really gets interesting. In Houston, Lorenzo White was always the last guy on the plane. He always missed the team bus, always was late to the airport, always showed up at the last second. Then, just before we shut the plane door, there he was, with a big grin on his face.

Once he was on time, but the players wouldn't let him on until after everybody else. "Bad luck," they said.

Same way, every week.

They also won't let Lorenzo on if he's not wearing his Mr. T starter kit. We knew we couldn't win unless Lorenzo White had on about $6,000 worth of gold. We're talking chains, gold medals, Mercedes Benz emblems, gold medallions, hubcaps, you name it. The more gold he had on, the better we played. One game, Lorenzo started to get on the plane and everybody just sort of stared. All he had on was just a couple of necklaces.

"More gold, man," somebody yelled.

Lorenzo vanished, then suddenly reappeared, radiating with gold from head to toe. *Now*, I thought, *we gotta chance to win this baby*. Lorenzo runs a lot better after he's been wearing all that gold, because when he takes it off, he can't believe he weighs only 225.

The Houston Oilers were mostly a boots-and-blue-jeans football team. Nothing scared me worse than when Jeff Donaldson, a fierce free safety, got on the plane wearing Italian shoes and quoof-bag pants, which you might say made him look a little "sweet." I mean, Jeff is a blue-jean guy to the core. He got on in that cute little outfit, and the whole team went, "Oh boy."

We got beat, 38–0. Now it's one thing to lose a game. But when you lose a game because of Italian shoes and quoof-bag pants, it's kind of hard to take. From that day on, we never made a road trip unless J.D. had on his 501 jeans. No more quoof-bag clothes for that guy. J.D. once wore the same pair of jeans every day for five weeks.

Nothing upsets me more, though, than locker rooms. No matter where we play, I want everybody to have the exact same space they had the last time we played there. In 1989, we played a preseason game at Dallas, where we had beat them four straight times. I walked in the door, and everybody was all over the place. Nobody was in the same place as the last four times.

I went nuts. I told the players and coaches to move back to where they had been the last time. We screwed it all up, though. A few guys moved, but some couldn't remember and the others were brain dead. Of course, we lost to Dallas that night for the first time in my career as head coach.

Food can win games, too. For instance, if we win, then the next week the coaches have the food brought in from the same place we ate at the week before.

We went on a three-game winning streak once that nearly killed me. I asked Linda Greer, my secretary in Houston, to bring the staff Blimpies sandwiches. Every day. For three weeks. Finally, we got beat and switched to Kentucky Fried Chicken.

"Jerry," Shive told me, "I hate to say this, but those Blimpies were starting to give me gas. You reckon that could have meant bad luck?"

Oh boy.

Haircuts are special, too. When you're winning, you can't get a haircut, because you don't want to cut any wins out of your hair. You just let those wins grow right on out there, over your collar, over your ears. You look stupid, but you feel good. Show me a guy with a great haircut and I'll show you a loser.

I'm pretty particular on the sidelines, too. Nobody hands me anything before the national anthem. Not my headset, not statistics, not the play sheets, not anything. Steve Watterson, who assists me on the sidelines, once handed me my play sheets prior to the national anthem.

"You trying to lose this game?" I said. So Steve sang real hard, which, of course, made up for the bad luck of handing me the play sheets too soon.

During the national anthem, I always made sure Kenny Johnson was standing next to me. One year he was on injured reserve, but we flew him to an away game for luck. I told him if we ever cut him, we'd have to fly him in each week for the national anthem. It's gonna be tough without him. And I never let anybody congratulate me until the game is completely over, regardless of the score or how much time is left.

On road games, I always make sure somebody's wearing my black high plains drifter jacket, which was handmade on the Indian plains in Wyoming. It doesn't even have to be me wearing it. Just as long as somebody's wearing the high plains drifter, we usually win. In the Astrodome, I always wore my big belt buckle, which was the driving force behind Houston's great home record from 1987–89. I've already got a new Falcons belt buckle, which is *twice* the size of my old Houston buckle. I also wore boots in the dome, but on the road, I wore coaching shoes.

Winning or losing also dictates the type of music I listen to. After a road trip, from the time we get on the plane, I listen to my CD player with earphones. If we win, I crank up the album *Lonesome Jubilee*, by John Cougar Mellencamp. As loud as it will go. And I keep listening to it for the rest of the week.

If we get beat, I listen to Jerry Jeff Walker all week. That guy brings me back. Every song is a story, it's all about real life and overcoming adversity. Recovery music.

But if you think I'm bad, you should see the players. Houston had a bunch of characters, but no one was ever worse than our punter, Greg Montgomery. There have been crazy kids, but Greg beats them all.

Let me explain. During the 1989 season, Montgomery was the caretaker of a giant stuffed rabbit that stood about four feet tall. Greg affectionately named him "Bugs," after the cartoon character. In the practice facility, Bugs even had his own locker. Every week, Montgomery would put a cutoff T-shirt on Bugs. He then would scrawl an obscene message on the shirt directed at that week's opponent. And for luck, he'd carry the rabbit every-where—home, practice, the Astrodome, everywhere. The rabbit really got to be strong luck; Bugs was responsible for at *least* two wins.

But by mid-October of that season, Montgomery made

a fatal mistake. Every Wednesday, Montgomery and the kicker, Tony Zendejas, would go to lunch with the offensive linemen at McDonald's. The two kickers would buy long-snapper Bruce Matthews lunch, then the other linemen would pitch in $3 apiece. Zendejas and Montgomery would purchase the food and serve the linemen.

But then the linemen realized something: The lunches were only costing Montgomery $2.35 each, which meant he was keeping the extra 65 cents per player, a profit of $2.60 a week.

"It's not the money," said Dean Steinkuhler, "it's the principle. Just the fact that Montgomery has been ripping us off all these years—somebody had to pay."

That set off a series of events that would drastically change our luck for the worse. The next day at practice, the offensive linemen took athletic tape and taped Montgomery from head to toe, turning him into a living mummy. Montgomery managed to cut the tape and escape, then snuck into the locker room and cut the linemen's chin straps and shoelaces.

"Insult to injury," Steinkuhler said. "The only way to get his attention was to take a hostage."

That's how Bugs became a victim. The linemen kidnapped him prior to the Pittsburgh game. At the time of Bugs's disappearance, he was wearing a T-shirt that simply read: "Chuck Noll," and he had a rolled pair of socks stuffed in his pants.

The next day, when Montgomery returned to his locker after practice, he found Bugs face down with scissors sticking out of his spine.

I don't play Chuck Berry quite as much as I'd like
  But I feel like Hank Williams tonight

But no amount of Jerry Jeff Walker will rationalize the actions of Cincinnati head coach Sam Wyche, who ignited the feud between the Oilers and Bengals. And that feud will carry over long after I've been forgotten in Houston.

When we went to Cincinnati with two games to play, the Oilers were in need of a single victory to clinch the AFC Central title. We had lost Dickie Byrd, Ray Childress and Robert Lyles to injury, so we knew we had a tough road ahead of us. But nothing could have prepared us for what happened in Cincinnati. Our quarterback fumbled away the opening snap, and boom, Boomer Esiason fired a 22-yard pass for a touchdown. I blinked my eyes, and the game was out of control. We trailed 30–0 at halftime.

Getting your butt beat is part of football. We've never complained about a good butt-whipping. But leading 45–0 midway through the third quarter, Sam called for an onside kick. The Bengals recovered and scored again. It was 52–0 going into the fourth quarter. We finally scored our first touchdown, but the Bengals kept throwing the football and scored again. With twenty-one seconds left in the game, Cincinnati called time out and sent out its field goal team. Bengals' kicker Jim Breech hit a 30-yard field goal, making the final score 61–7.

After the game, Sam opened his locker room to the press and began a verbal assault on our football team. "The Oilers just got embarrassed and humiliated, and I would hate to ride that plane back home," Sam told the media. "They are a sorry football team. They play stupid football. His [Glanville's] teams have no discipline, and when you have no discipline, you have trouble winning. They are the dumbest, most stupid, undisciplined football team we've ever played, and it's hard to believe they can ever win games."

When I heard Sam's comments, I was stunned. I didn't know where he was coming from. I didn't know what precipitated it. Sam was a guy I respected. When I was an assistant at Detroit, Sam was one of the most emotional, hardest-working players we had. Now he's calling me a phony. I thought that was funny—most people say I'm too honest, that I say what's on my mind.

What was interesting, though, was that the week before we played Sam, he had grabbed a microphone and taunted the Cincinnati crowd for throwing snowballs. Then, after the Bengals *lost* that game, he closed up his locker room and wouldn't talk to the press. But when they beat us so bad, he talked to every reporter in America. I think if you really want to show how tough you are, close your locker room after a *win*, not after a loss.

I'm surprised that the guy who called the Oilers "the most undisciplined team in football" was the same person who had lost to us five out of the last six times. We set our standards pretty high. Our standards are so high, in fact, that a lot of people don't like us. And because they don't set their standards as high as we do, they accuse us of not playing within the rules.

In the NFL, you have to be very careful when you

criticize anybody else's team for being stupid, for being undisciplined, or for hitting late. Because as soon as you start pointing fingers, or criticizing another team, the next Sunday you'll line up and your team will lose the game doing those same exact things. Sam blasted me and the Oilers for those things, then the next week the Bengals got knocked out of the playoffs making the same mistakes.

When I got home after the Cincinnati loss, I went upstairs to my TV room. There, on one of my shelves, was a game ball from 1974, when Detroit had beaten Cincinnati, knocking the Bengals out of the playoffs. The Lions had awarded a young coach named Jerry Glanville that game ball. It was an emotional time for me and the players. Especially for a backup quarterback named Sam Wyche, who presented me with the ball. He said, "Jerry, we couldn't have won without you."

The NFL is a small world.

But let's face it. Coaching is fun. That's why I do it. And it certainly beats working. For every bad moment, there are a million good ones. Like the time I walked across the field after the Oilers beat the Cowboys to shake Tom Landry's hand. During his career, Tom never was good with names. Right when he got to me, he glanced down at the palm of his left hand. He had my name *written* on his *hand*. He says, "Great game, Gary."

Gary? Who's Gary? I felt like saying, "Thanks, Fred."

My wife and I got to know Tom and his wife real well when we went to dinner during the week of Super Bowl XXIII. His wife asked me how long I'd been coaching.

I said, "Twenty-six years." She said, "You don't even look twenty-six years old." From then on, I've been a great admirer of hers. The thing I remember most about that dinner, though, is that Tom ate just like he coached—he left nothing to chance. He chewed every bite of food at least thirty-eight times. You could see him counting. Tom would've had a hard time where I grew up. In Detroit, you had to eat fast or somebody else would steal your food.

Some people believe that coaching in the NFL is a science, but I disagree. It's a people business. There is no set way to win. Different personalities work for different teams. The biggest differences between winners and losers isn't the head coach, but the assistant coaches. I was an assistant coach most of my adult life. When you spend a long time as an assistant, you learn to appreciate the foot soldiers, the guys in the trenches. I've learned more from the assistant coaches I've worked *with* than the head coaches I worked *for*.

The league needs more characters as head coaches. Guys who don't take themselves so seriously. Some people don't like Philadelphia's Buddy Ryan, but I do. I've never talked to Buddy Ryan for more than five minutes, but it's obvious that he's his own man. He does things his own way. Most people don't know that Buddy Ryan lied about his age when he was a kid so he could enlist in the army to fight for his country in Korea. He was jumping out of helicopters with machine guns and wasn't even old enough to be there. That makes me respect him. But you never hear him talk about that.

One of Buddy's former assistants, Ted Plumb, worked with me the first time I was in Atlanta. Ted is known around the NFL as "The Man Who Wouldn't Let Buddy Die." Buddy was choking on a piece of meat once, and Ted jumped up and saved him. Mike Ditka's never forgiven Ted for that.

I was amused when Jimmy Johnson accused Buddy Ryan of putting a bounty out on some of the Dallas players. When I saw the film, I thought it looked more like a mutiny on the bounty. I was surprised anybody ever brought it up. I can't imagine an NFL coach putting a bounty on another team's players. The only bounty I ever heard about involved former Duke quarterback and TBS analyst Ben Bennett. He was playing Arena Football, and an opposing team put a case of beer on his head. Unfortunately, Ben drank it.

Sometimes I wonder what kind of car Jimmy Johnson drives. I bet it has lots of chrome. I've always said that chrome is for coaches who use hair spray. I've never seen Jimmy with a hair out of place. He has to learn that to win in the NFL, you can't keep cutting wins out of your hair. Jimmy must get a haircut twice a week. He needs to let it grow, especially after a win. You never get a haircut after a victory.

For that same reason, I think Jack Pardee will win at Houston. Jack won nine games with the University of Houston in 1989, and never got a single haircut. The problem was, you couldn't tell.

Mike Ditka is another character. But the Oilers turned on Mike after our game against them in 1989. We scored two touchdowns in the final minutes to beat the Bears, but Ditka infuriated our players after the game by not giving them any credit for the victory. I can remember Alonzo Highsmith saying he always respected Ditka until he made the remarks he did after that game. I talked to Mike before the game, and he was very complimentary to our players and coaches.

After the game, however, Mike ridiculed our football team and talked about how horrible the Bears must have been to lose to the Houston Oilers. A lot of people don't think his heart will take much more, but the real question is, How much longer can his assistant coaches last on the same sideline with him?

Cleveland's Bud Carson is pretty special to me. I'm glad I'm out of that division, because now I can root for him.

Kansas City's Marty Schottenheimer is another guy I root for. When I left Houston and was out of work for a week, Marty cared. He called me immediately. His wife called my wife. Those are things you don't forget. I've kidded Marty in the past for his liberal use of Vince Lombardi quotes, but when times were tough, he was there for me. He understood my problems at Houston, because he suffered through the exact same thing at Cleveland.

What's funny is that Seattle coach Chuck Knox told me two years ago what would happen to me at Houston, and to look forward to it. He predicted what would happen to me *before* I left Houston, and Marty predicted

As a senior in high
school.
(Courtesy of author)

Back in the early years
of coaching.
(Courtesy of author)

Note that I need a haircut. Show me a head coach with a good haircut and I'll show you a coach with a losing record. *(Courtesy of author)*

e of the few times you'll find me in a edo—and Brenda d Justin wanted a picture of me for posterity. ourtesy of author)

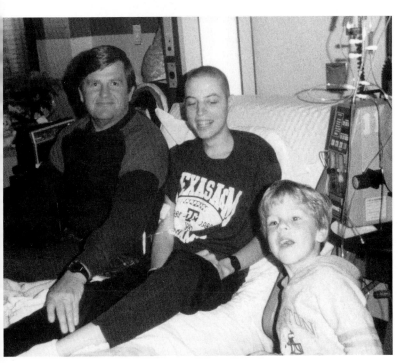

I always find time to visit football fans, no matter where I am or what I am doing. Here Justin and I visit Adam Kulik in Anderson Hospital on Christmas in 1987. (Courtesy of author)

Justin will have to start wearing Atlanta's colors now. *(Courtesy of author)*

One of my favorite possessions. Need I say more? *(Lou Witt Photography)*

I've always taught "smash-face" football, and it turned the Oilers' fortunes around. *(© SPORT Magazine)*

Exhorting the troops when I was at the helm in Houston. *(Pizac Photography)*

The man in black is always in the center of the action. *(© SPORT Magazine)*

Most of the time, the zebras and I get along pretty well. Except when they're rookies. *(Courtesy of author)*

NNESSEE	OPERATOR		LICENSE		
LICENSE NO.	EXPIRATION DATE	HEIGHT	WEIGHT	EYES	HAIR
571459	01 08 77	600	170	BL	BK
S	DATE OF BIRTH	ISSUE DATE	CONDITIONS		
M	01 08 35	09 18 75	5		

```
PRESLEY ELVIS A
3764 ELVIS PRESLEY BLVD
MEMPHIS                    TN   38116
```

Elvis A. Presley
SIGNATURE OF OPERATOR

Want proof that Elvis lives? Here's his Tennessee driver's license. *(Courtesy of author)*

If you play for me, you've got to play hard-nosed, rock 'em, sock 'em football. No "Lassies" allowed. *(The Houston Post)*

The eye of the storm. And guess who's there? *(Tom J. Moore, Sr.)*

what would happen to me *after* I left Houston. Both guys were right on the money.

Another guy I respect is Joe Gibbs at Washington. Fans don't realize it, but his teams always play better than the ability of the players he has. Joe has spent half of his life around a projector and a chalkboard. I heard that when a relative of his got married, somebody asked Joe what he thought about the wedding ceremony. "I don't know," he said. "I haven't seen the film yet."

My favorite coach to watch is Bill Parcells of the New York Giants. He has to be the toughest guy for NFL Properties to market—they're still trying to find clothes that he looks good in. But Bill is close to the bone. What you see is what you get. His shirttail is always hanging out, he's very superstitious and he eats his way to the playoffs. And he never, ever cuts any wins out of his hair. In fact, he seldom combs it. Bill reminds me of my close friends.

Perhaps the best part about coaching in the NFL, though, is the heartwarming relationships you develop with officials. Nothing is more special than a conversation with an NFL referee. In 1989, the Oilers were playing Dallas in a preseason game. The officiating was some of the worst I'd ever witnessed. I was seething on the sidelines when Ben Dreith walked past me.

"Hey, Ben," I yelled. "You've stolen everything else from me tonight, so here, you may as well steal my watch, too."

Somebody had just given me a brand-new $15,000

Rolex. I ripped it off my wrist and threw it at him. Dreith calmly walked over, picked it up, then put it on and walked away. I quickly came to my senses.

"Hey," I screamed, "bring my watch back."

If Ben wasn't such a jerk, I'd consider him close to the bone. Ben won't let you hit the quarterback. Of course, to be fair, he won't let your quarterback get hit, either. One time we were playing Cincinnati, and the Bengals ran a sweep. We were bearing down on the halfback, and just as we hit the guy, the halfback jumps up and throws a pass. Ben penalized us for roughing the passer. Unbelievable. Ben Dreith finally retired. I had great battles with him; sometimes I wasn't real proud of things I told him. But Ben could get to you like nobody else could. I remember one game distinctly where I called him over to the sideline.

"You're terrible," I said. "You stink. But you're not alone. I'm doing a worse job at coaching than you are at officiating. But I'm gonna try to do a better job, if you'll do a better officiating job."

Ben looked at me. "You're really not doing that bad a job, Jerry," he said.

I didn't criticize him the rest of the game.

The guys who upset me the most are the rookie officials. NFL football is a vastly different game than it is in college, where there is so much boola-boola garbage. A rookie official is like a rookie player. They shouldn't be allowed to make decisions, they should just watch. They really cause problems. Every time we have a rookie official, I tell him to be good to us, it's our homecoming.

One time we were playing Chicago in the Astrodome, before they had the crowd-noise rule. The Bears were the world champs and we were a struggling young football team. Chicago got the ball down close to our goal line on a bad call, and the place erupted in boos. A rookie official came over to me.

"According to the NFL commissioner, you have to come out on the field and wave your arms and quieten this crowd," he said.

I said, "Let me tell you something. The only guy this crowd hates more than you is me. If I come out on the field and start waving my arms, it may start a riot. We're in the middle of losing eight in a row. Somebody might get killed if I get out there."

The referee thought for a second.

"Good point," he said. "I think we'll let the noise just sort of die down on its own."

My coaching career is marred by two regrets. The first is that I never met George Halas or Vince Lombardi, who to me were the greatest coaches ever. My other regret is that I *have* met so many of the guys who are coaching now.

When Papa Bear Halas retired, people couldn't believe it. Somebody said, "You own the team, you run the team, you coach the team, why stop coaching now?"

He said, "Because last Sunday when I chased an official down the sideline, I wasn't gaining on him."

That's when it's time to get out.

11

Snakebites, Gator Bait and a Dog Named Rusty

Being a head coach in the NFL doesn't make you invincible. I learned that lesson halfway through the 1989 season, right before we played Pittsburgh for the first time that year.

It all started when my wife Brenda wanted to go for a bicycle ride with Justin. It was late on a Saturday afternoon, and I didn't have a team meeting for several hours. So I put on my flip-flops and spandex shorts and jumped on my bike and we took off. We'd ridden about a block when we came up to a house that was under construction. It was already framed and looked magnificent. Brenda wanted to check out the inside. So we got off our bikes and marched through some knee-high grass and into the house.

When we walked out of the house, I deliberately turned to my son and told him to step carefully in the high grass. There were several boards lying around with nails sticking out of them, and lots of tools and equipment in

118

the grass. Most importantly, because we lived right on a lake, I told him to watch for snakes.

Justin, who was seven at the time, turned to me and said, "Well, Dad, if that's true, then why don't *you* have on shoes?"

Ah, the wisdom of a child. About that time, I was stepping over a couple two-by-fours in this thick grass. Suddenly, I slipped on a block of wood and felt a sharp sting in my right foot. Instinctively, I reached down and grabbed at the top of my foot. When I looked at it, I couldn't imagine how I had flipped this two-by-four upside down and driven two nails into the top of my foot.

When I reached down to pull the board off of my foot, there was nothing there. When I got to my bicycle, there clearly were two unusually deep holes in the top of my foot. I tried to squeeze the holes to make them bleed, but they wouldn't bleed. Neither hole would bleed.

By this time, Brenda and Justin had ridden about a half a block. I finally caught up with them.

"Brenda," I said, "look at my foot."

Now my foot was solid red at the top, and my big toe was red and swollen. It looked a lot like Dan Dierdorf's nose.

"What happened?" she asked.

"Something bit me."

"Don't worry about it," she said. "When we get home, I'll put some bug stick on it."

So we turned our bikes toward home. Halfway back,

we ran into Herb, one of my neighbors. Herb took one look at my foot and nearly fainted.

"Jerry, you've been bitten by a snake," he said. "You better go to the hospital immediately."

I laughed at him.

"I promise you, Jerry, that's what it is."

Herb suggested I go see Sam Power, another neighbor who is a big hunter and fisherman. Sam lived out in the woods all the time and was the local expert on outdoor injuries. Personally, I don't know a bite from a sting— I'd rather watch paint dry than hunt or fish.

So I rode my bike four more blocks to Sam's house for his diagnosis. His reaction was the same as Herb's. "Jerry," he said, "that's a snakebite."

Jo Ann, Sam's wife, still didn't believe it.

"Oh, don't worry about it," she said. "I'll spray it with Bactine."

By now there were big blotches around my ankle, big squares that looked like age spots. My foot was tingling, like there was an electrical charge in it. The shock would go away for a minute, then it would come back twice as strong.

So we decided to call poison control. They switched us over to the people who handle snakes. We described the symptoms to the man on the phone. He ordered us to go to the emergency room immediately.

I said, "I don't want to go over there and it turns out not to be a snakebite."

Jo Ann put ice on it, and Sam and I got in his car and headed to the hospital.

We pulled up at a red light, and all of a sudden, it was like a bolt of lightning hit my foot. I said, "Sam, you better run this light, because my foot feels like it's about to drop off."

So we took off. About four minutes later, the pain quit. I told Sam to slow down. Five minutes later, the pain hit again. This went back and forth until Sam was ready to shoot me and put me out of my misery.

When we got to the emergency room at Southwest Memorial Hospital, I suddenly realized that I had neglected to change clothes. I had on no shirt, no shoes, and spandex pants. When I wear spandex pants, I don't wear underwear. I've never liked underwear, anyway.

The attendant came out, took one look at this half-naked forty-eight-year-old man in spandex pants with a fat foot and smiled broadly.

"Don't I know you from somewhere?" she asked.

I introduced myself as Chuck Noll.

"I have a problem with my foot," I said.

She was more concerned about my insurance than my foot.

I said, "I think I got bit by a snake."

Sam said, "I think he was bitten by a snake."

Finally a nurse came out and said, "I think you've been bitten by a snake."

I felt like asking, "Who's on first?"

They took me into the back room and put a heart monitor on me and started drawing blood. The doctor finally came in and told me they were calling snakebite people in Arizona and Florida. Meanwhile, they monitored my heart and blood pressure and gave me a tetanus shot and an antibiotic shot. They confirmed that I had been bitten by a snake, but they said they would have to wait twelve hours to see if I needed the antivenom shot.

With the shot, I'd be in the hospital for three days, because your joints swell up and your body swells all over. The doctor said it would be a very unpleasant experience, even worse than playing in Cincinnati.

The other alternative was to hope that the snake had eaten recently.

"If he's eaten recently," the doctor said, "then he won't have enough venom to hurt you. If he hasn't eaten within seventy-two hours, then you have to be put on antivenom. If we determine he has eaten something, then we will have to treat you for whatever it was he ate."

Eventually, they figured my snake had just eaten a rat, or some other vile form of life. So I had to have tetanus shots in the butt because of this snake's diet. As it turned out later, it *wasn't* a rat. It was a Houston newspaper columnist.

Somewhere in the middle of this ordeal, it occurred to me that we're playing Chuck and the Steelers the next day. So I told the doctor, "Look, I have to get out of here. It's 5:30, and I've got a team meeting at 8 P.M."

He said, "You can't leave. I really don't care if you die, but I'd lose my license."

So I got the team doctor on the phone, who agreed to take care of things for the next twelve hours. But I still had to sign a waiver stating that the emergency room doctor was not responsible for me and that I agreed to stay on crutches for two days.

"Jerry," the doctor pleaded, "just stay until midnight."

I said, "I really can't. I have a team meeting." What I didn't tell him was that Jerry Jeff Walker was meeting me in my hotel room after the meeting, and that he was gonna pick and sing for me and my coaches right there in the room. You can't miss Jerry Jeff over a snake, especially one that has been hanging out with local journalists.

I signed the waiver and met with the team doctor. By now the hospital tests had determined that the snake had been a water moccasin. Then our team doctor informed me that 17 percent of the people who go on antivenom die. Now *that* was good news. I said, "Where am I— have they already lost their 17 percent today? I want to know—am I the first guy today or the last?"

I went to the team meeting, caught Jerry Jeff back in the room, and then finished up the game plan with my coaching staff. Brad Brown, Houston's trainer, put me back on crutches and took me over to St. Joseph's Hospital for more blood tests about 1 A.M.

The doctors there told me that if my blood didn't coagulate, then I had the venom.

On Sunday, I woke up early to go to church. I looked at my arm, where they had taken blood for tests. My arm was solid black and blue.

I said, "Ohmygosh, I'm not coagulating."

I went to church on my crutches. Internally, I felt like I had a touch of the flu. The foot hurt, but not too bad. I even stayed on the crutches until I went to the stadium. I'd done everything I had been asked to do.

By the time we came out for the first half, I was covered with cold chills.

I asked Red, the Oilers' equipment guy, for a T-shirt to put on under my shirt. He didn't have one. I asked him for a sweater; he didn't have one. I asked him for a jacket. Nope.

The team doctor suggested I take a couple of the steroid-based healing agents we keep on the sidelines. So I got in the steroid dose bag and took six of them. I didn't know that it's the strongest medicine we give out. I chased the pills with a couple of Diet Cokes.

I hadn't eaten all day. I was freezing. Our ace staff didn't have an extra sweater, jacket, or anything. And I've just dropped six pills on an empty stomach.

The next thing I knew, I had to vomit. Bad. The doctor took a look at me and said, "You need food." So he sent somebody up in the stands to get me a hot dog.

Meanwhile, the Oilers and Steelers are slugging it out on the field in the second half. I, on the other hand, was on the sidelines eating a hot dog. Imagine how Chuck must have felt when he looked over and saw me eating a hot dog, with mustard running down my chin, right in the middle of a game.

By Monday, I felt okay. On the following Tuesday morning, I woke up scratching the snake bite. The fang marks had risen way up above the skin. It was very red. The doctor sent over some antibiotics to put on the actual bite. On Wednesday, my body temperature dropped two degrees, and I stayed wrapped in blankets. I had the chills and was as cold as I've ever been. It was the last struggle, the last fight. I'd heard maybe it was in my lymph glands. The doctor even suggested at one point that it might be the medicine, not the snakebite, that was making me sick. Whatever the case, by Thursday, I was fine. The holes, however, stayed for quite a while.

I'm the luckiest man in the world. The fang bites were over a half-inch apart. How many guys who get bit by a snake that size are lucky enough that the snake had just eaten?

Somebody asked me how I could get bit by a snake in my own neighborhood. Well, neighbors told me they saw Chuck Noll driving around that house just minutes before I was bitten. And a couple of days later, my neighbor Jo Ann found a four-foot water moccasin in her driveway. She hit it with a shovel. The snake had a big lump right in the middle of it, where it was still digesting something, like a newspaper. I sympathized with that poor snake. A Houston newspaper can kill anything.

Chuck Noll said my snakebite sounded like a family argument. Hell, for Chuck to say something humorous, really, he ought to go in the Hall of Fame for that comment. I've always wondered what Chuck would've said if he'd been with me at the time and I asked him to suck the venom out of my foot.

I think he would've looked at me with compassion and said, "Jerry . . . goodbye."

A month later, we went to Pittsburgh to play the Steelers in a snowstorm. The fans tied rubber snakes to long strings and dangled them down over the tunnel where we ran out. Fans are great.

I've also received about twenty-five snakebite kits in the mail. Jerry Jeff Walker said he's gonna get me a pair of water moccasin boots. In fact, my bootmaker, David Wheeler, is making me a pair of cattle-hair boots with a water moccasin on the side. Truth is, if I had actually seen this snake biting me on the foot, I would've died of a heart attack. But as quick as I put my hand down there, I never saw a snake, or touched a snake.

But having snakes loose in my old neighborhood in Houston was really boring compared to the other excitement around there. People thought that was crazy—hell, we had an 8-foot alligator that lived in our backyard. I lived in Sugar Lakes subdivision, in Sugarland, Texas. Everybody's house was about 25 feet off the water. The lakes have been there forever. Oyster Creek, which is famous for alligators, feeds into Sugar Lakes.

I nicknamed our alligator, who regularly roamed the banks, Sparky. One evening Brenda and I were visiting the Kennedys, some friends of ours down the street. We were sitting on their back porch, looking out over the water, talking about the fact that just two days prior, Justin had fallen into the water behind their house. While we were talking, I happened to glance out there, and right off their dock was Sparky.

I said, "Look at the size of that thing."

Jim Kennedy looked at the gator and then back at me.

He said, "You know what, let's shoot that thing."

I said, "Yeah, I'll go get my weapon."

Now Jim lives on the other side of the water from me. I went around to my place and got my .357 Magnum. When I came back outside, Jim hollered, "It's right by you."

Jim's wife turned on the floodlights. I found Sparky hiding under my next-door neighbors' dock. So I got on their dock and started jumping up and down. That sucker exhaled with a roar, his tail smacked the water and he submerged with a rush. I guarantee you, he scared me twice as much as I scared him.

Meanwhile, my neighbor came running out. He'd never seen an NFL head coach jumping up and down and waving a .357 Magnum before.

"What in the world are you doing out here?" he said.

I said, "I'm hunting Sparky."

He got all shook up that we were in his backyard hunting an alligator. The next thing I know, the game warden sends me and Jim a note wanting to know why we were hunting alligators in our neighborhood.

The letter insisted that I couldn't kill an alligator unless it was a life-threatening situation. Well, I grew up in Detroit and I know how that game goes. I figured once I shot that gator I'd just drag him in my kitchen and put a biscuit in his mouth and a knife in his hand.

A few days after my neighbor kicked me out of his yard, lo and behold, his big wire-haired terrier named Rusty disappeared. Sparky loved dogs. Another neighbor had already caught him trying to get his Irish setter. And now the same neighbor that got shook up over me hunting the alligator lost his dog. He insisted that Rusty had run away.

I say Rusty was dinner.

Rusty always wore flea collars. So I bought a couple flea collars, and for the next few days, I'd throw one in the lake and let it float down past their house. Then, when I'd see my neighbors, I'd ask them if there was any word about Rusty's whereabouts. They'd sniffle and shake their heads.

My son and I really are not the outdoors type, which is evident by the fact that he fishes off our dock and uses hot dogs for bait. He catches these big soft-shell turtles. He catches so many that it's like somebody told them that some kid was fishing with Coney Island hot dogs— word gets around, even with turtles.

There was a monkey in the neighborhood, too. He used to belong to somebody, but he escaped and ran wild around our neighborhood like a miniature Sasquatch. One night he was screaming and crying. I thought, "Maybe Sparky . . . was tasting a little monkey."

That monkey was wild, all over the place, like Jay Schroeder on a bad day. One day my son came in and described this thing he and his friends had seen swinging through the trees.

I looked at him with disbelief. "Son, you just described *Houston Chronicle* columnist Ed Fowler."

He assured me that, no, this was a *real* monkey, not just someone working hard to be one.

For months, the kids would see the monkey swinging

through the trees, hooping and hollering. I figured it was only appropriate that we had monkeys in the neighborhood, to go along with the gators, turtles, snakes and dogs.

But one thing is certain: The snake that did bite me hardly compared to all the other "snakes" I avoided during my six years on the job with the Houston Oilers.

12

If You Don't Like Me, I Probably Didn't Like You First

Before I resigned in Houston, somebody read me this quote, which they attributed to ESPN analyst Pete Axthelm:

> Jerry Glanville is the best thing to happen to the
> NFL in 20 years. In a couple years, the Oilers
> will be in the Super Bowl and Glanville will be
> the hottest thing going.

That's real nice. But it proves that Pete will say anything for $20. What I like about Pete is that, like us, he knows how to have fun. He showed up in Houston one time to do a story on our special teams wearing an army helmet. Our players got a big laugh out of that.

"You are really crazy, Jerry," Pete said.

Here's a bald, middle-aged, TV reporter, wearing an army helmet with a coat and tie, and he's telling *me* I'm crazy?

"We need to be a little crazy," I told him. "It keeps most of the wimps who cover our games away from us."

Pete laughed pretty hard. My wars with the Houston press were highly publicized. But people don't realize that my problems were only with a few reporters. All I ask from reporters is just write the truth. I don't expect everything to be positive, just so it's true.

Dealing with the press is one of the most important jobs any head coach has, because what people see on television or read in the paper often shapes their opinion of your team, your coaches and yourself. It has a trickle-down effect. The problem is, you can't please everybody. So every day is another trial-and-error effort to try to keep things positive in the press.

Understand that there is nothing wrong with criticism. Criticism and controversy are part of the game. But if the media attacks me personally, attacks my family and attacks my team, that's when I fight back.

One problem in Houston was that, during 1986, my first full season as the head coach, we finished 5–11 and at one point, lost eight in a row. We were improving as a team, but our record was horrible. You can understand why I was a little sensitive. The entire time I was the Houston head coach, my job was rumored to be in jeopardy. My replacement, according to everybody, would be Jackie Sherrill, the former Texas A & M head coach who is a personal friend of Oilers' owner Bud Adams.

I'm convinced that if we had had a winning season in 1986, the media never would've been quite so vicious.

But once it started, there was no way to stop it. And when we did improve in 1987, '88 and '89, a few writers could not admit that they had made a mistake. So there was simply no way to resolve the issue. But 1986 was one of the longest years of my life.

Training camp in 1987 couldn't come soon enough for me. I knew we had a good football team, and I was eager to prove the critics wrong. Maybe that's what prompted me to call a truce with the press. I told the media that I was instituting my "Hug-a-Reporter Day" program, and I did, in fact, hug a few necks. I considered buying them all vacation plane tickets, but when I checked with the airlines, they had first-class tickets and coach-class tickets, but they didn't have no-class tickets, so we couldn't do it.

By camp, rumors were already flying around that if we didn't improve drastically, Sherrill would be the new head coach. One sweltering August afternoon, we had been practicing about forty-five minutes when a helicopter landed right on the field. Out jumped Jackie Sherrill. It was a very short practice that day. Of course, the columnists went crazy on their keyboards, thinking the axe was about to fall.

I asked Jackie how he handled the media at Texas A & M.

"I used to take them all out on a boat," he said.

"Well, I need a boat and about nine anchors," I said.

We *did* improve, dramatically, and marched to the playoffs that year. But if you go back through the Houston papers, you'd never know we were a playoff team. The

New York Times came to Houston in December that year to cover a bowl game and discovered Houston was in the playoffs. They were so stunned they wrote a story about us.

We upset the Seattle Seahawks in overtime in the wild-card game. It was Houston's first home playoff victory since the AFL-NFL merger in 1970, and gave us the right to play Denver in the second round of the playoffs. Reason to be excited, right? Wrong. The next day in the paper, two columnists wrote that the Seahawks "didn't deserve to be in the playoffs," and that the victory meant nothing.

On the following Tuesday, Kurt Iverson, a reporter from the *Dallas Times Herald* asked me if I wanted to say anything to the so-called "negative" media.

"Yeah," I said, "I'd like to book a grudge match in the Astrodome between me and the two Houston columnists. Problem is, I'd get arrested for child abuse—and those guys would be too scared to get in the ring with me."

That week I gave the players T-shirts that had an Oilers helmet facing a globe, with a "vs." in between. Us against the world was the basic message, because nobody expected us to make the playoffs. On the back, the shirts had an Oilers armadillo climbing steps to the top rung of a Super Bowl trophy.

Reporters asked me to define the meaning of the shirts.

"Of course I believe we're going to the Super Bowl," I said. "You're not going to beat Denver if you don't think you're going to beat Denver."

Never has a single quote been so misconstrued. My

one comment, meant to motivate our players into believing they could win the game, was totally blown out of proportion. It was first reported by Houston papers as "Glanville predicts Houston Victory Over Denver." As the story zinged its way around the country on the national wires, it was seen in the following forms: "Glanville Slams Broncos"; "Glanville Says Houston Better than Denver."

But what was I supposed to say? That Denver was 10–4–1 and that we didn't have a prayer against the likes of Elway and Co.? The crucifixion continued all week, right up to game time.

Fittingly, our biggest breakdown of the year would come in a game that had been hyped bigger than life because of my single misconstrued statement. Six minutes into the game, I sent in a play named "Stagger Lee," which called for a staggered formation in which tailback Mike Rozier lines up wide left behind three offensive linemen.

The object of the play was for the quarterback to read the defense and make one of three choices. One of those was a long lateral pass to Mike Rozier, which had resulted in long gains twice during the regular season. Denver was in the perfect defense—man-under zone—for the play. We were backed up to our own 5-yard line, and my assistant coaches agreed that Stagger Lee would totally surprise the Broncos.

Everything looked perfect. Except Mike dropped the ball. Just dropped it, doink, right off his pads. Denver's Steve Wilson recovered the fumble at the 1-yard line, and two plays later, Gene Lang scored to give Denver a 7–0 lead.

We committed ten penalties, suffered another fumble and threw two interceptions. Final score: Denver 34, Oilers 10.

Predictably, the media went absolutely crazy ripping me over Stagger Lee. An example:

> It's called Stagger Lee, but on the sunny turf of
> Mile High Stadium, it wasn't nothin' but a hound
> dog. If optimism were gold, Glanville would be a
> walking Fort Knox. But if brains were made of
> that precious commodity, he couldn't fill a tooth.

It seems some reporters wouldn't root for their own mothers if they were flying into the Houston airport on a plane that had two engines out. It would be a better story if the plane crashed and burned. I feel sorry for people who have to get up every morning, slap their kids, eat breakfast, and then charge out into the world to find something negative.

Our football team improved, but nobody noticed. We beat the Browns in Cleveland in the first round of the 1988 playoffs and came a touchdown away from the AFC Championship. And in 1989, we made the playoffs for the third straight year, tying Houston with Cleveland as the AFC's *only* teams to make the playoffs three straight years. Still the papers clamored for my firing.

In all fairness, I must say that Houston has two of the best reporters in the NFL. Guys like Ray Buck and Kenny Hand really bust their butts to do a good—and fair—job. They weren't always positive, but they were honest.

Sometimes I think the media would like twenty-eight coaching clones. But my stint in Houston taught me not to care what the media says. It would bother me if the press thought I was a great coach and my peers didn't think I could coach. The bottom line is that the media can't save your job if you lose and it can't get you fired if you win.

One Detroit reporter, Curt Sylvester, told me that I dodge a lot of bullets. I don't. Not really. When it comes to the media, I'm really bulletproof. I just go out and be myself. I don't want to do anything more than win games. My motto: Be yourself and go to work. If you worry about trying to win over the media, you're not doing your job.

Some people think I don't have any friends in the media, and that's not true, either. There's lots of guys out there I have a lot of respect for, like Axthelm. After Pete interviewed me in 1989, we both got into my 1950 Mercury and rode off into the sunset. He said, "Where are we going?"

I said, "Moscow, Idaho, will be our first call home."

When I was a youngster in high school, one afternoon a friend and me were feeling just a little crazy, so we jumped into my '55 Ford to go for a ride out of Perrysburg, Ohio. When we finally called home, we were in Moscow, Idaho. It was a very long trip—we didn't even have a change of clothes.

I really like Bob Costas, John Madden, Ahmad Rashad, Marv Albert. Great, funny guys. At least they have personality. And in Bob's case, when he was critical of the Phoenix owner during the 1989 season, at least he had the courage to face the man. Bob has way too much courage to ever work in Houston. Costas and I have never been big friends, but I owe him one. He defended me when few people would, and I'll never forget that O.J. Simpson is good, too. His advantage is that he doesn't always pass on the left. For that reason, we agree. Maybe all the time. He's a guy who likes to deviate from the norm.

When it comes to announcers, my personal favorite is NBC's Bob Trumpy. The reason I think he's so good is that he actually knows the rules better than the officials do. He actually knows what's going on. Plus, he does what Madden used to do—that's come in prior to a game and do homework and study. I remember when Madden broke in, he came in three days prior to a game to study and learn the teams and the players. A few years later, he started coming in two days early. Now, you're lucky if you get a phone call. As big and as large as he is, he's become invisible. But no one compares to Trumpy. No one is more correct, more studied about the game. As a coach, that's what you appreciate. I'd rather hear Trumpy than Bill Walsh, whose knowledge of the game is probably more than twice what the fans can comprehend. But because of his sense of humor, however, he needs that knowledge.

How can anybody *not* like ESPN's Chris Berman? He's alive and exciting. I like that. He's not a mundane, droning bore. When you meet him in real life, it's shocking.

He's 9 feet tall, but when he sits behind a desk he looks 5 feet 5. In Houston, he set a world record for sweating. He tried to interview our players once and changed his shirt six times. He'd never make any money doing a deodorant commercial. But I love the guy.

Another fun guy is NBC's Paul McGuire, who loves his job so much he doesn't realize he isn't any good. Paul knows how to laugh along with you, and unlike most reporters, he doesn't take himself seriously.

And who in heck is Fred Edelstein? What has Fred ever done with his life, except eat a 92-ounce steak and a dozen donuts at one sitting? I put Fred in the same category with Bobby Beathard and Ralph Wiley. They're nice, straightlaced little guys, who sometimes have to skirt the thin line of objective journalism in order to generate controversy.

My prediction is that if San Diego isn't in the playoffs in 1991, Bobby Beathard will be fired. My reasoning is based on the simple fact that Bobby said that about me one day on NBC to make news. I called him and asked for his source. He claimed that somebody in the Houston organization said I would be fired. He says it was somebody higher than me, but not as high up as Mr. Adams. That only leaves one person, which is Mike Holovak, and Mike says he never talked to him. Do you think Mike Holovak would lie?

I think that Bobby Beathard was so boring he tried to become something through shock television. So, for the record, I predict he'll be fired in San Diego. Who could believe a man who wears tennis shoes without socks, anyway?

Ray Buck wrote a column one time that really summed up my feelings about the media. In regard to all the people in the press who think I'm a jerk, Ray wrote that ". . . if you don't like Jerry Glanville, he probably didn't like you first."

Funny that a reporter said it better than I ever could.

13

Livin' Close to the Bone

"Just Because I'm Middle-Aged Don't Mean I Like
To Sit Around and Watch TV"*

A song that I really identify with is John Cougar
Mellencamp's "The Real Life," on his *Lonesome
Jubilee* album. In the song, he talks about real
people, tough people, people who live close to the bone.
Almost all of the players and coaches who stick with me
live close to the bone. There is a shortage of players like
that. I still have a love affair with blood-and-guts football
players. I'm tired of pretty boys who are afraid to get
dirty. I still love the guys who prefer to run over you
instead of around you, who understand that pain is a
friend, not an enemy.

I think people who live close to the bone are people
who only answer to themselves. Not people who try to

*"The Real Life," *Lonesome Jubilee*, John Cougar Mellencamp, © 1987
Riva Music

impress other people, but people who live day to day, always fighting for what they believe in. When you live close to the bone, you set your own standards and strive to meet them. Like President George Bush. He is definitely his own man. Before he was elected, President Bush called me in Houston during the middle of a practice. One of our equipment guys, Bill Lackey, who we called Mojo, took the call.

"I'm sorry, Mr. Vice President," Mojo said, "but Coach Glanville doesn't come off the field for anybody but Mr. Bud Adams."

Mojo told me later that he saluted during the entire conversation.

Imagine my embarrassment when I discovered what Mojo had told the Vice President. I tried to call him back, but I was unsuccessful. I think at the time he either wanted me to be his press secretary, since I was so close to the media, or he wanted me to help write Dukakis's campaign material, which would have eliminated Dukakis even faster.

Close to the bone means you dress however you want to, say whatever you have to say. People may criticize you, but you couldn't care less. Most of the coaches who have criticized me are just mad because they don't have as much hair under their headsets as I do.

When you live close to the bone, you either bring out the best or the worst in people around you. I think that's why so many other players and coaches get up for my football teams. Other coaches, other cities get excited when we come into the stadium. They love for us to be there. The Pittsburgh crowd, the Cleveland crowd, the Cincinnati crowd.

When I look around the league, I don't like players based on where they were drafted or who their daddy is. I like players and coaches who live close to the bone. I think close to the bone isn't clear-cut to the fans. It's how I perceive these guys because I've seen them from the sidelines. And Lord knows, I may see a player differently than everybody else sees him. But I've learned that a close-to-the-bone player, the guy who becomes your all-out player, comes from different parts of the country, comes in all shapes and sizes, dresses in all different ways and wears all different kinds of hairstyles. I don't see many of them that don't wear socks. But no matter what package he comes in, the close-to-the-bone player never surrenders, regardless of the score.

Take quarterbacks, for instance. Pittsburgh quarterback Bubby Brister is a fierce competitor. He's a linebacker pretending to be a quarterback. He's got toughness, he's got courage. If you don't like Bubby Brister, you don't like football. I've never spoken to him one time, but I can tell by the way he plays that he lives close to the bone. Bubby Brister is what you want your guys to be. Sometimes I think he might throw an interception just so he can hit the guy who picks it off. Against Denver in the '89 playoffs, Pittsburgh ran a reverse. Bubby threw a devastating block that took out *two* defensive linemen. He is absolutely fearless, the kind of guy I'd like in my huddle.

Buffalo quarterback Jim Kelly is another one. Kelly should've been thrown out of several games when I coached against him at Houston. In 1986, we had a fight break out against Buffalo in the Astrodome. Referee Ben Dreith came over to me.

"The next guy who throws a punch is out of this game," he said.

I said, "Fine, Ben, but go tell the Buffalo coach."

So he did. A few plays later, Kelly threw an interception. Allan Leyday intercepted it and started running down the sidelines. Kelly made the tackle, and as both players were getting up, Kelly wound up and hit Leyday with an uppercut right in the mouth. *Wham*, just smacked him.

I went crazy. I ran up to Ben Dreith, screaming.

"You said the next guy that throws a punch is out of the game!" I bellowed.

"Not the quarterback," Ben said. He pointed up in the stands. "You see this crowd?" he asked.

I looked around. "Yeah," I said. "Big deal."

"If I throw out Jim Kelly, there won't be anybody at this game but you and me. Kelly stays."

I thought that was pretty unfair. Kelly can throw punches, but nobody else can. But I like him. If Jim Kelly wasn't playing football, he'd be a policeman. A thug with a badge. But he'd have to be an undercover cop, because he's too sloppy a dresser to wear a uniform.

Tampa Bay's Vinny Testaverde is rapidly improving, and he's nearing Kelly's level. He throws the streak route better than anybody, and throws the slant like Dan

Marino. But Vinny needs time. He's not quite there yet. Another guy I like is Boomer Esiason. I admired Boomer before anybody else knew who he was. For a left-handed guy in a right-handed world, Boomer is incredible. I picked him to be the player of the year before the 1988 season. That was the only time I said something exactly right. But like Vinny, Boomer still hasn't reached his peak. I think Boomer is somewhat handicapped by outside influences. I love the guy, but I don't think he realizes who his true admirers are.

I respect Bernie Kosar because he's got the best mind in the game. Fans don't realize that Kosar is the best at looking one place and throwing another. And when you look at his passes, you realize he needs that advantage. But his passes aren't as bad as his stance. The way Bernie stands under center, it's like John Wayne riding sidesaddle. But Bernie makes great decisions. And he's got the courage of Dick Butkus. When Bernie's out of football, he'll take a job where decisions are critical, like working on my income tax.

Steve Beurlein is by far the Raiders' best quarterback, but they won't admit it because they traded for Jay Schroeder. They can't admit that Beurlein is the best quarterback because it would make Jay look bad. But Schroeder's at best the second-, or maybe third-best guy they've got in Los Angeles. Beurlein is dirt tough, but he's a project. But anytime you have toughness, that's a plus.

Terry Bradshaw calls John Elway the biggest baby in the NFL, but he obviously never had to coach or play against him. John's always played brilliant against us. I saw him have a bad day in Super Bowl XXIV, and I wondered why he never played like that against our teams. I stood on an elevator once next to him at training camp. I was shocked at his size; he was so much bigger than I imagined. He reminds me of a tight end.

A guy that's still a mystery is Jim Everette of the L.A. Rams. We had Jim in Houston, but traded him to the Rams. After the trade, he said he thanks God every day that he didn't have to play for us, that he was thankful to go somewhere where he could get good coaching. After we played against him twice, it was obvious he needed *great* coaching. We whipped him twice. The Rams are a Super Bowl contender, but I think it's got more to do with John Robinson, Ernie Zampese and Flipper Anderson than it does Jim Everett.

Receivers are harder to judge. But a guy that catches my eye more than anybody else in Cleveland's Webster Slaughter. Everybody knows he has great ability as a receiver. But what people don't know is he may be the best downfield blocker in the league. He's hard nosed, he's tough and he'll fight at the drop of a hat. Webster Slaughter would play fullback if he had the size—he loves contact, which is a rare trait in a receiver. I also think his ugly orange shoes make him a little faster. I like those shoes, but they're not original. I took my son to the circus once, and some fat guy with red hair and a red nose was wearing the exact same shoes. Another great receiver is Buffalo's Andre Reed. He's as good after the catch as anybody playing, and that includes Jerry

Rice. I think Andre Reed is the most underrated receiver in the game.

You've heard us talk a lot about courage, and that is absolutely a prerequisite in running backs. You can't be close to the bone without courage. I love Walter Payton because I never saw him run out of bounds, I never saw him give less than 100 percent, regardless of the score. I watched him when Chicago was a terrible football team. The Bears would be trailing by 40 points, and they'd hand Walter the ball on the last play of the game, and he'd still try to score. That's a special guy. You can't even compare Walter Payton and Franco Harris. Franco would've been a great player in Canada, because the field's wider. NFL sidelines weren't wide enough for him. Don't tell me about yards rushing or touchdowns, tell me about courage.

I guess that's my problem with Bo Jackson. I admit that Bo has great acceleration—he hits the hole faster than anybody in football, except for maybe Sylvester Stamps, who plays for the Tampa Bay Buccaneers. When I was in Houston, our game plan for Bo Jackson was to take away the sweep. We worked on it all week. Then, after about three plays, we scrapped the game plan and decided to take away the *inside* run, because Bo was coming up the middle like a freight train. He killed a week's worth of work in three plays—he got at least 30 yards in his first three carries.

But I've also noticed that Bo Jackson doesn't play much. I wonder if he misses as many quarters as he plays? Sure, Bo can hit the home run, but we can't have a guy who won't play every down. Our running backs don't leave the game when they get a little boo-boo here or there. Mike Rozier, Alonzo Highsmith—those guys *never* ran out of bounds. They punished you. Alonzo Highsmith is a strong, fast tough guy with a great attitude. He's really not a natural, gifted athlete. But he has such a great mental makeup, and he works so hard, that he has made himself into one of the best fullbacks in football. Yes, I'd take Alonzo Highsmith over Bo Jackson.

Eric Dickerson is a thoroughbred. The second year I was the head coach in Houston, we opened against the Rams in the Astrodome. They got in a formation where I knew it was a weak-side pass. So we called a weak-side blitz—we sent everybody. But instead of passing, they gave the ball to Dickerson. He blew past me on the sideline like a scared antelope. I'd never seen a guy that big run that fast. Somehow we dragged him down at the 4-yard line. We won that game, but only because of Jim Everett.

A lot of people don't like Eric. I read where he says he hates to get hit, and I admit, he does fumble occasionally. But if I had Eric Dickerson, he'd be carrying the football until he didn't want it anymore. I can only judge him by the games he's had against our teams, and, like Walter Payton, I've never seen Eric Dickerson give less than 100 percent.

When it comes to offensive linemen and tight ends, we've had a couple of special guys that would easily make my All-Bone team. While I was in Buffalo, we had a center named Will Grant. He was a beauty. Grant would hold, grab, cheat, lie and steal to win a game. He's the kind of guy you want on your team. He won a game for us against the Colts by spitting in Barry Krauss's face. Barry retaliated and was penalized, and it cost them the game. Grant was mean and dirty, he fought every day in practice. It was hard for me to love the guy, though, because he drove a yellow Eldorado. To me, he always seemed like he should be driving a black '57 Buick.

Six-foot-five, 250-pound Jamie Williams played tight end two years for us in Houston. He was definitely close to the bone. He had a ponytail that hung down his back, and he dared opposing players to give it a tug. "I'm afraid that if any player should pull my tail during a game, there will be an awful fight," Jamie told me once. Jamie, who owns the entire *Spiderman* comic book collection, believes he is the reincarnation of Spiderman. "I really identify with Spiderman, the way he conquers bad guys," he says.

Defense, of course, is the closest thing to my heart. But they just don't make defensive players as close to the bone as they used to. The first time I coached in Atlanta, we had two defensive linemen named Jeff Merrow and Jeff Yeates. We nicknamed one "Bone" Merrow and the other "Dog" Yeates. Bone and Dog talked a lot, had bad bodies and overall weren't very pretty. Every Sunday we had the "Dog & Bone Show." Both of them probably ran a six-second 40, but they were incredible for three hours every Sunday. We used to play "Take It to the Limit One More Time," in the locker room before games, just as loud as it would go. And they did.

One year we were going to play Seattle. The night before the game, Yeates went to some hamburger buffet and got some guy at the buffet to bring a couple cases of beer up to his hotel room. He drank them all. It wasn't that tragic, except that he called his wife up and talked to her all night, long distance, while he drank the beer. He finally passed out with the phone lying next to him. His phone bill at the hotel surpassed his salary.

By the start of the game the next day, he didn't look too good. I was in the press box when suddenly I heard Yeates's voice on the phone. I looked down on the field, and there he was, dehydrated, ghastly-looking, barely able to hold on to the telephone on the sidelines.

"Sticky," he said, "I promise you, if you don't make me play this game, I'll never drink again."

I said, "Yatesy-dog, you're gonna play every single snap."

"Coach," he said, "if you leave me in there, I'm going to get very, very ill. I'm gonna puke, Coach, I'm serious."

I said, "If you're going to vomit, do it on the Seahawks."

He did. Before the game was over, he threw up all over the entire right side of the Seattle offensive line. Now that's what I call close to the bone.

The starting nose tackle at Houston was Richard "Dickie" Byrd. I called our defensive line "Dickie Do and the Don'ts." After training camp in 1988, I started calling Richard "Puke," because that's what he did. Every single day. One day, Puke came up to met after practice.

"Coach," he said, "I don't mind being called 'Puke,' except in front of my family. If *you* don't mind, when my family's around, just call me 'Vomit.' I'd appreciate it."

Wow. That's close to the bone. I loved Dickie Byrd and Ray Childress, because they only knew one speed— wide open. Dickie used to fight in practice all the time, and that was a real treat. It was a special sound to hear Dickie's fist colliding with somebody's helmet. Finally, I fined him. Not for fighting, but for hitting people's helmets.

"Dickie," I said, "I've told you over and over: If you get in a fight, punch the guy in the stomach. I can't have you breaking your hands."

When we look around the league at other defensive linemen, I think Reggie White of the Eagles is a close-to-the-bone kind of guy, too. He says what he believes, he doesn't care if you like him. He gets extra points, too, because his shirttail is always hanging out, and he's always got a little stomach showing. That's good bone material. On the other hand, William "The Refrigerator" Perry has too much stomach. He's not half as good as his younger brother, Michael Dean, who plays for Cleveland. Michael Dean comes hard every down. William can't play a half without stopping for a bucket of chicken.

Linebackers can fool you. If they weren't basically nasty individuals, they wouldn't be linebackers. But just being a linebacker doesn't qualify you as being close to the bone. Neither does a bad haircut. The Boz—Brian Bozworth—is a good example. He has declared himself a champion, which makes bad players play great against him. I don't know what his real personality is. What bothers me about Boz is that he hasn't been on the field in so long, I forgot how to spell his name.

Don't get me wrong. Haircuts don't bother me. Anybody who coaches Jamie Williams, who is now a tight end with the 49ers, learns to love haircuts. Woody Hayes taught me that a long time ago. He was the first guy who won games with players who had long hair and wore high-heeled shoes. He told me that his only injury one year was when somebody fell off their platform shoes. I always thought Woody was *the* disciplinarian, *the* consummate general. But Woody made it clear he didn't care if you looked like a girl, just don't play like one. There's a big difference.

An example of a good haircut is Clay Matthews, the Browns' outside linebacker. He's had an unbelievable career. He's not only been around forever, but he's probably played in five different defensive schemes. It doesn't matter whether he's playing on the line of scrimmage, or stacked behind the line, or whatever.

I'll never forget the game Matthews played against us in 1985. He was rushing, trying to get a sack, then reached out to club a running back and broke his arm. He never quit running—he did a full 360-degree turn, ran over to the bench, slammed his helmet down and told the trainers to fix him. It was obvious the kid's arm was totally broken. But Clay made them tape him up. They ended up putting a pin in his arm between seasons, but he was right back the next year, breaking face masks. He's a special guy. I always loved the guy because he plays special teams, too.

With linebackers, you have to press different buttons to get them motivated. In Houston, we used to motivate Eugene Seale by telling him if he made a great hit, we'd give him a big bag of potato chips. Family size. He was so round in 1988 that we nicknamed him the "One-Man Gang." But in 1989, he ate so much that we started calling him "Two-Man Gang." One time Eugene grabbed me before a game.

"Coach, can I let my whole personality come out?" he asked.

Reluctantly, I agreed. He lasted six seconds. He ran down on the opening kickoff, ripped the ballcarrier's helmet off and punched him right in the mouth. Boom. They ejected him immediately, six seconds into the game. It was the quickest ejection in the history of football. It looked like a Floyd Patterson fight—it was over before anybody sat down.

I told Eugene, "You've now become the first NFL player to be ejected in six seconds. That's the last time I want to see your whole personality." I believe in aggressive football, but not if it makes us play shorthanded.

Another linebacker we love is Scott Studwell of the Minnesota Vikings. He just won't retire. You see him in there all patched up, nose bleeding, elbows bleeding, eyes bugging out. That's a football player. He's so old, he doesn't shave anymore. But Scott thinks he's getting younger.

Defensive backs were always my favorites. To this day, there's nothing I appreciate more than a good defensive back. Cris Dishman in Houston is going to be a star. He took a lot of criticism for taking a bow after an interception when Cincinnati beat the Oilers, 61–7, but I don't see where a good bow hurts anything if you've done something good, regardless of the score. Red Skelton always took a bow after every great performance. If you've made a great play, and you can take the criticism, take a bow. Usually the people who complain about showboating are the ones who didn't play hard enough themselves. Dish tries to rip your head off. We tell our players, "If you want to showboat, that's okay, because that means you can't take a single play off."

In Dish, we see a guy who may also be one of the all-time great people to ever play in the NFL. A guy who, when practice is over, hurries to get dressed so he can walk fifth-graders past the crack houses without them getting in trouble. On Tuesday, his day off, he visits kids with AIDS, kids whose parents won't go near them. In Cris, I see something different than what Minnesota or Pittsburgh sees. He doesn't care what people think, because he knows who he is and where he is going. He isn't interested in your opinion. That's a big man in my book. If Dishman ever needs a home, he can ring my doorbell.

I've also been blessed throughout my career with unbelievable safeties. In Detroit, we had Charlie West; in Atlanta, Ray Easterling, Tom Pridemore and Bob Glazebrook; in Houston, Jeff Donaldson and Bubba

McDowell. Kenny Johnson played for me in Atlanta and Houston.

Pridemore and Glazebrook are still special to me. The impressive thing about Tom Pridemore was that he was a little guy, but he didn't know it. He hung around with real big guys, offensive and defensive linemen. If they drank a lot, he thought he should. I think those linemen took a lot of years out of him, they shortened his career. What's funny is he almost never got a chance to play.

During his rookie year, Doug Shively always called Pridemore a freshman. He looked so damn young sitting on the bench. Then one day we were in a crucial game with the Rams, and Ray Easterling, our starting safety, went down with an injury. We sent the freshman in.

The next day, I trudged in to work, still sick over Ray's injury. Shive was smiling. I said, "What are you smiling about? We just lost the best safety in football."

"Wait until you watch the films," Shive said.

That taught me that you never really know what you have on the bench until you see them play. I looked at the film, and Pridemore was incredible. As a rookie, he helped get us in the playoffs. He never dodged anybody.

Glazebrook, meanwhile, had unbelievable athletic ability, but he had no speed. He could shoot hoops, play tennis, drive a golf ball, and was drafted in baseball, but he couldn't beat his mother in a footrace. So we had to figure out a scheme where we could use his athletic ability and toughness without isolating him one on one. We played him more as a linebacker than as a safety. Glaze and Pride were the original Bruise Brothers. They were a big reason the old Atlanta Falcons lived right on the edge.

When I arrived in Atlanta, the first thing I tried to do was get Jeff Donaldson, Kenny Johnson and Tracy Eaton—all three of my safeties from Houston. At one time, Jeff Donaldson was as close to the bone as a man can get. He's another overachiever. For three years, Jeff was as good a tackler as there was in the league. I get excited when I think back to Thanksgiving Day 1988, when Houston played the Cowboys. J.D. went head-to-head all afternoon with Herschel Walker and won every single time. All day long, that's all you could ever hear from the bench: Herschel left. *Whap.* Herschel right. *Whap.* Great collisions.

When Donaldson was younger, Houston was playing Pittsburgh, and the Steelers were breaking the trap on us pretty well. This was back when Steelers running backs didn't avoid anybody. But they would bust it up through the hole, and boom, J.D. would meet them head-on, going full speed in the other direction. He just splattered people for sixty minutes. That day, Jeff was in a class by himself. That was Houston's first win in Three Rivers Stadium, and they could thank J.D. for it.

When I was at Houston, we found Tracy Eaton playing at Portland State. Just before the 1988 draft, June Jones was looking at one of their running backs on film. By accident, he happened to watch a little defense. He yelled, "Jerry, you better look at this." I couldn't believe this kid—he was an absolute trained killer. During a game against Pittsburgh, he punched a guy in the mouth, and the guy bit him. Tracy was wearing gloves, and the guy bit right through his gloves. When Tracy showed me the bite, I ordered our trainers to check him for rabies.

Of all my safeties, though, Kenny Johnson's my favorite. He goes wherever I go. Nobody in the history of football loves to play and practice the game more than Kenny Johnson does. He belongs in a special place in the Hall of Fame, he is a legend, right up there with The King. In fact, Kenny Johnson may *be* the bone. The first year I coached him, he weighed 155. After the 1989 season in Houston, he weighed 194, and that was after the thousands of hits and blows he's taken over the years. Yet he's still the first one down on kickoffs. I remember one game where Kenny was ejected for biting a guy on a kickoff return. As usual, Kenny denied he did anything wrong.

That's the beauty of coaching players who live close to the bone. They're never guilty of anything.

14

"Taking Every Wrong Direction on My Lonely Way Back Home"

I remember it like it was yesterday. Nearly 60,000 Houston Oilers fans were on their feet in the Astrodome. We were locked in a wild-card playoff battle with the upstart Pittsburgh Steelers, who behind good coaching and the leadership of quarterback Bubby Brister had somehow managed to get in the playoffs. And, unlike many Steelers teams of recent years, this Pittsburgh club refused to die. We were in overtime, and the Oilers were driving, and all we needed was a field goal to put this thing away and head to the showers.

For a long time, I'd referred to Houston running back Lorenzo White as "East-West," as in East-West Shrine Game. "Lorenzo plays like he's still in college," I'd joke. "He loves to run East and West instead of North and South." I was only kidding. But with the Oilers driving toward that winning field goal to advance us in the 1989 playoffs, my worst fears became reality right before my very eyes.

We pitched out to Lorenzo. Instead of turning it up,

he saw pressure and tried to outrun it toward the sideline. Give credit here to Steeler defensive back Rod Woodson, who really smacked Lorenzo right in front of our bench. It was like the entire season was reduced to two seconds of slow motion. I can still see Woodson flying in, head down, putting his helmet right on the ball. Lorenzo's face was screwed up in a tight grimace. The ball began to come loose, then trickled down his right leg.

Finally, there it was, loose, no more than 2 feet from me. I wanted to dive on it, cover it, protect it. My stomach was in my throat. A horde of Steelers covered the ball. Four plays later, Pittsburgh kicker Gary Anderson ended our season with a 50-yard gunshot that would've been good from 60 yards.

I'd said it a million times before, but never was it more true than at the end of the 1989 season: Nowhere else can you experience the highest of highs and the lowest of lows than by spending a year in the National Football League. Like that, boom, it was over.

As I trotted off the field, a million things were racing through my mind. I saw many Houston players openly weeping as they walked off the field. I was proud of that. When I arrived in Houston, it didn't bother the players to lose. But now, the Oilers had tasted winning, and anything short of victory no longer satisfied them. I was also crushed for Lorenzo White. There are few players in the NFL as competitive as he is. He would've given every penny he's earned in the league to have that fumble back.

After the game, for the first and only time, my son crawled up in my lap and cried. He whispered in my ear, "Dad, I'm really proud of you." I knew what was coming next. I knew what the reaction of the vultures would be. As I held my son, I asked God to protect my family for the next ten days.

The tension in the front office at Houston after our third playoff loss was obvious. In my heart, I felt it was time to move on. I asked Houston general manager Mike Holovak for his permission, in writing, to talk to other teams. So Mike went off and got it in writing. My next step was to call Atlanta to see if they would interview me. Atlanta, at the time, was hotly pursuing someone else, an NFL assistant coach.

"We can't talk to you," Falcons vice president Taylor Smith told me. "You're under contract."

"Taylor," I said, "I have a letter that says you can."

He said, "We'll have to talk to Mike Holovak."

Taylor called Mike, who granted his permission, then he called me back. "Mike says it's OK, but bring that letter with you anyway," Taylor said. "We're not getting in any trouble over you."

When I boarded the plane in Houston, I was greeted by a *Houston Chronicle* photographer, which surprised me. Nobody but Bud Adams and Mike Holovak knew I was going to Atlanta. Word got back to Atlanta, and when I got off the plane in Georgia, there were more reporters, who asked me what I thought about Atlanta.

"If you're not sleeping in Atlanta, you're just camping out," I said. That's an old Civil War statement, which I had picked up in 1968 while studying Civil War history.

Now, everybody knows I love Houston and I love

Texas. But when you come back home you're glad to be there. But some of the Houston media, as usual, made more out of a statement than they should. The bottom line was that I was happy to get a chance at the Atlanta job.

I interviewed with Rankin Smith, Jr., Taylor Smith and Falcons' personnel director Ken Herock for more than nine hours. It was the first time I'd ever been in a hotel room with three other men for more than nine hours without taking a shower.

During the interview, they asked me if I had studied Atlanta's talent and what I thought of each position. I told them, "I just got done coaching a playoff game, and I haven't even looked at a single player on this team." It was an unusual year, that in all the film exchange, I never saw the Falcons on film one time. I told Ken Herock I didn't really care what the personnel was. I think you learn that the longer you're in the league, players are going to change, but owners don't. You learn that there is a plan on how to make yourself a good organization. I saw how Kenny Herock had planned to build the organization, how he planned to orchestrate Plan B free agency and developmental squads, and I realized that I was being cheated in Houston.

I told them that I wouldn't evaluate the players, I wouldn't judge them. If a player had the very best year of his career in 1989, that didn't mean beans. But if he had his worst year, that guy's not in trouble either. I told them I'd like to start at point zero. I told them, more than anything, I was concerned about ownership, management and—something that is lacking in a lot of organizations—trust.

They seemed positive, but after the interview I didn't think I had the job. It was the first time in my coaching career that I interviewed for a job and didn't believe in my mind that I would get it. I got back on the plane and went back to Texas, frustrated and unsure about my future.

When I got home, Brenda could tell by my face I wasn't thrilled. "I've never seen you after an interview when you didn't think you had the job," she said. "What happened?"

I explained that Falcons' owner Rankin Smith, Sr., had never appeared for a minute during my interview. Having worked in Atlanta in the past, I knew you had to meet with Mr. Smith in order to be the head football coach.

Meanwhile, I found out that while I was in Atlanta, the Houston press and ESPN were declaring that I had been fired for camping out in Atlanta. Mr. Adams, however, defended me all the way. He told the press, "Jerry's my coach, and that's it." But two days after I got back from my first Atlanta interview, I called Mr. Adams and asked him for a meeting.

The first thing he asked me was, "Have you heard from Atlanta?"

I said no.

He said, "Well, I did. I talked to Rankin Smith, Jr. They're really interested."

For the next two hours, he asked me what I would do to make the Houston Oilers a better organization. Mr. Adams wrote down everything I told him on a yellow legal pad.

After two hours, he drew a line underneath all the things I'd told him. Then I said, "Now write down that I don't want to be a part of it. I don't want to be here. I want out."

Mr. Adams looked hurt. "Is there anything I can do to change that?"

I shook my head no.

Then Mr. Adams called in my lovely bride and talked to her about it. Brenda was torn up over the whole thing. We had settled in Houston and made a lot of close friends there. But it was obvious that it was time to go. Some people thought I left because Mr. Adams wouldn't give me the authority I wanted. But I didn't ask him for anything. I didn't ask for an extended contract, I didn't ask for any more control or money, I didn't ask for anybody else to be fired.

"Maybe I'm not right," I told him. "Maybe I'm making a mistake. But this is my opinion."

"Jerry," Mr. Adams said, "Why not just ride this thing out? Why not stay one more year?"

Again, I shook my head no. I told him I didn't want to be fired, I didn't want to quit, I just wanted us to mutually agree to go our separate ways. And I thanked him for his undying support and loyalty during my tenure in Houston.

Finally, he agreed to let me out of my contract.

He said, "What about money?"

I said, "Give me ninety days' pay and ninety days' hospitalization. I'll find a job in ninety days. I'm not after your money. I just need to move on."

I left $300,000 in salary sitting on the table. Brenda looked at me like I was crazy. But I've never been afraid to roll the dice. We set the press conference for that afternoon, one week after we'd lost to Pittsburgh.

Mr. Adams got tears in his eyes at the press conference. "Jerry can stay if he wants to stay," he said. Then the national media, of course, reported it as a firing. Leave it to reporters to screw up the facts.

Monday came and went, and my phone still hadn't made a sound. By that time, I had conceded to Brenda that I probably didn't have a job. "Honey," I said, "I've messed this thing up. I think we've made a big mistake."

Brenda said, "Call Atlanta." I said, "No. If we're out, we're out." My son, Justin, asked me to call the Raiders. I asked him why, and he said, "because that Bo Jackson can really run. I like Bo Jackson." My son still doesn't understand why his daddy can't coach anywhere he wants to.

By Thursday, the only people who had contacted me were the folks of ESPN. They wanted to know if I had any interest in broadcasting. Disappointed that I hadn't heard from any football teams, I told them I'd make arrangements on Friday to fly up for an interview.

I never got the chance. On Friday morning, Falcons' vice president Taylor Smith called me and asked me if I could fly to Atlanta Saturday. I said, "Is your dad going to be there?"

Taylor said, "He'll talk to you Saturday. We'll send a private jet to pick you up in Houston."

"How big is it?" I asked.

"It holds seven people," Taylor answered. "Why? Are you bringing Brenda and Justin?"

I said, "No, I'm not. But I am bringing all my boots and hats, and that'll take up half that jet."

My son and my wife drove with me in the car, out onto the runway. The pilots loaded up fourteen pairs of my boots, three straw hats and two beaver hats, lots of black pants and shirts and three pairs of Wranglers.

We took off. I had my CD player cranked up. I was listening to Jerry Jeff Walker and Kris Kristofferson all the way to Atlanta. I wasn't in a good mood, and I thought those two guys could bring me back.

When I landed, I had on boots and a straw hat and my high plains drifter jacket. They put me in the hotel under a fictitious name. It's funny, because reporters told me they checked every hotel under Elvis, James Dean and Jerry Jeff Walker. The people who really knew me even checked the name John Cougar Mellencamp. Truth is, I was under the great name of Smith.

We went in the back door of the hotel. Everybody on the elevator recognized me. I stayed in the room and waited. And waited. And waited. Taylor finally called me late that night and said, "We can't see you today, but we'll see you in the morning."

The next morning, Taylor came to pick me up. My

picture was on the front page of the newspaper, along with a headline declaring me as the next head coach. People I didn't even know at the hotel came up and congratulated me.

Taylor just smiled the whole time. We drove over to Mr. Smith Sr.'s house, which looks like Tara, maybe bigger. When they swung the iron gates open, my jaw dropped. I got out of the car, and I heard Mr. Smith say, "Jerry," but I couldn't see where he was.

He called about three times, and I finally saw him standing in the garage. Right then I realized one reason why I liked this guy so much, because he was standing between a red Rolls-Royce and a Ferrari. Anybody who loves cars, especially fast ones, is a friend of mine.

He said, "Welcome home."

I followed him through his 15,000-square-foot antebellum home. I said, "Mr. Smith, if we don't sell any tickets to the games, I know we could sell tours through this house."

We walked through the foyer, and I expected Rhett Butler or somebody to step out and, quite frankly, I'd give a damn. This house is a page out of history—just walking through it, I lost track of what year we were in and why I was there. I was really fascinated by the woodwork. Finally, we sat down.

Mr. Smith said, "Jerry, I don't want anybody else in America to coach this football team except you."

He stuck his hand out. "I think a handshake beats a contract any day. I'm offering you this job if you want it."

I put my hand out. "What's in our hands, a man can't write on paper," I said. "I want to be your coach."

He said, "That settles it. You're it."

We shook hands firmly. Mr. Smith turned back to me. "Jerry," he said, "I've got two questions to ask you. Where does Brenda want to live? And where do you want Justin to go to school? Those are my biggest concerns."

I told him we'd figure it out.

What impressed me was that Mr. Smith didn't ask me to win any games, he didn't say you have to go 8–8 or 9–7. He just said, "The last time you were here, I had great pride in this football team. This city was proud to be Falcons fans. I want great pride in being the owner and I want the city to be proud of this football team." From the time I shook his hand, I told him, that would be our direction.

So he called a press conference. Mr. Smith got up and introduced me to the local media. Kenny Herock told the media that after the first interview with me, he didn't want anybody else. "A lot of other teams might have steered clear of Jerry because of his controversial reputation," Kenny said. "But his philosophy doesn't bother me. In fact, his kind of football agrees with what I'm trying to get done here in Atlanta. Jerry gets a lot of his ideas from back in the old Raiders days."

Kenny, a former Al Davis protégé himself, reminded the media of the days when the Raiders "hated Pittsburgh and we hated them. That's the style Jerry has. I knew that he was the kind of guy that I wanted to take out there on Sunday to see if we can beat the 49ers, beat the L.A. Rams."

The reporters all wanted to know how many years I would get on my contract and how much I would be paid. I said, "I don't know, but what we have is something a lot of organizations don't have, and that's trust."

Mr. Smith trusted me with the job, and I trusted him to take care of me. Rankin Smith Sr. may be the best thing that's ever happened to me, period. Every coach in the NFL has skeletons in his closet. The beauty of my situation in Atlanta is that the Smith family knows all my skeletons and still wanted me as the head coach. They know I may have been the only coach in the NFL that rode to work on a motorcycle for ten years. They know what really is me and what isn't.

Amazingly, Mr. Smith ignored all of the negative stuff that had been written about me. "The worst thing a man can do is listen to somebody who hasn't been in the arena," Mr. Smith said. "Why would I listen to somebody who hasn't accomplished anything? I'm hiring Jerry Glanville, and I'm hiring the total package. I know what's inside Jerry Glanville, and I know what I want."

A week earlier, the Houston media was ready to tar and feather me. They pointed to the Oilers' poor finish, and particularly, our defeat in the playoffs. The Atlanta press, taking a page from the Houston reporters, asked Mr. Smith if he was bothered by my three playoff losses.

"I remember we had that same problem here in the late seventies," Mr. Smith replied. "If that's a problem,

I hope Jerry brings those problems back to Atlanta with him."

Ken Herock elaborated on that. "The Oilers went to the playoffs three straight years under Jerry," he said. "The Falcons have never had three straight winning seasons. The playoffs—that's the criteria. All this other crap doesn't count."

The "other crap" Ken was talking about was in regard to my run-ins with Sam Wyche and Chuck Noll. But after my appointment in Atlanta, even Sam and Chuck seemed more diplomatic. "Jerry works as hard as anybody in his business," Sam said. "We disagree in philosophy, but anybody in this business knows the ups and downs that you go through. Jerry is a guy that can get it done as well as anybody else."

Wow! What a difference a few weeks makes. I almost thought maybe somebody needed to take Sam's temperature.

After the press conference, Mr. Smith said, "Jerry, I'd like you to be the head coach until the day I die." I immediately thought I'd find me a good nurse to make sure he didn't get sick for a long time.

I couldn't believe how I felt that Sunday night. That night, when I went to bed, I couldn't sleep. I was absolutely wired. I was also *afraid* to go to sleep, for fear that when I woke up I'd still be the head coach of the Houston Oilers. Once again, I felt like the luckiest man alive. It was obvious that the good Lord had heard my prayers to protect my family for the next ten days.

The day after my hiring, I left with Ken Herock for

the Senior Bowl. I never went back to Houston. I jumped right into my new job. My wife started handling the packing on her end, and I started getting ready for the 1990 draft. The day I resigned in Houston, I had started eating like a horse, and I didn't quit eating until the press conference in Atlanta. I had lost about 25 pounds at the beginning of the season, and then, like I do every year, I ate my way to the playoffs. This time, I ate my way into a new job. It felt great.

Everywhere I go in Atlanta, people say, "Welcome home." If I was the head coach in New York or Phoenix, it wouldn't be the same. Maybe I'm the right guy in the right situation in the right place. When people in the South say "welcome home," they mean it. I've got roots here. My wife was born in Atlanta, my son was born in Atlanta, my dog was born in Atlanta. In my book, that makes me a native.

After I took the job, my son called every day and asked for Neon Deion Sanders's autograph. So the first thing I did as the head coach of the Falcons was get Deion's autograph and mail it to Justin. When Brenda tried to put it in a wooden frame, Justin got upset. "No, Mom," he cried, "Deion only looks good in *gold*."

But everything wasn't rosy. The romance with Houston officially ended when several of my former Houston assistants tried to get out of their contracts to come to Atlanta. Houston vice president Tommy Smith called in Oilers' strength coach Steve Watterson and special teams coach Richard "Perfect" Smith and asked them, "Why? Why would you want to go with *that* guy?"

Steve told him, "Loyalty is a two-way street. This guy would do anything for you when you work hard for him."

The day the Houston Oilers hired Jack Pardee as the head coach, my old staff was told to look for work. Five days later, when I was named the Falcons' head coach, the Oilers rescinded all permission for the assistant coaches to talk to other teams. This has nothing to do with Jack Pardee. It just shows you that the Oilers' organization didn't expect me to be hired.

Ray Sherman, our receivers coach in Houston, came with me to Atlanta immediately because his contract was up. So did Doug Shively, who will be the assistant head coach in Atlanta. Shive has been with me so long that I don't think either one of us could work without the other.

Every year we won at Houston, I didn't ask for a 5-cent raise, but I did try to get my assistant coaches longer contracts and more money. I fought for that, and now here I am in Atlanta without most of them. You move on, but that feeling for those people never leaves you. When I think of Steve Watterson, I can feel his spirit every day like he's in the same room with me. Houston can't change that, they can't take him away from me. People like Watterson and Perfect become a piece of you. I think my body is a collection of people, a collection of relationships. You don't have to be in the same bunkhouse to feel their spirit. Without question, I learned who my friends were through this experience.

Nothing makes a head coach more proud than when other people chase after your assistant coaches. In 1989, a week after San Francisco beat Cincinnati in the Super

Bowl, the 49ers tried to hire Ray Sherman. We had two other guys get major college interviews. I take pride in the fact that somebody besides me recognizes what a great job my coaches do.

What's amazing is that some of these guys were laughed at when I hired them. I nearly got fired for hiring June Jones into the league. June had been a USFL assistant, and was a strong believer in the run 'n' shoot. Most NFL coaches insisted it would never work in the big leagues. Today, there aren't enough run 'n' shoot coaches to go around. When June left, I hired Kevin Gillbride from East Carolina State to maintain our offense; people around the leagues fell down on the floor laughing and kicked their feet in the air at that one. Another coach called me and said, *"East Carolina State?* Are you serious?"* Today, Kevin Gillbride is one of the brightest young offensive minds in pro football.

I hope they come after our coaches every year, because that means we're doing something right. All of our coaches are involved in the game, they all are a part of play selection; no guy is separated or told what to coach. Nobody is too special. We all work for ourselves and each other. I think loyalty is something nurtured through working together during hard times. It's sharing any good or bad thing that happens. When good things happened, we shared it with everybody. We were all dirt honest with each other, everybody was involved, and every coach contributed to his phase of the operation.

Any coach who has ever worked for me understands that, with me, your word is your word. Take June Jones, for example, who is now coaching the run 'n' shoot in Detroit. There isn't a more loyal man on the face of the earth. I hope my son has as much undying loyalty for me as June does.

June left Houston in 1989 to go work with Mouse Davis, whom he played for at Portland State. I can understand that. Mouse was his mentor. He told me later, "Jerry, you had the guts to hire me, and I'll always love you for that." I'm lucky that I've had people like that.

By the same token, you may be the best assistant coach in the history of football, but if you're not loyal, then you're not with me. When somebody breaches their word, that's it with me. Ask Ted Plumb, who is now an assistant at Phoenix. We worked together for three years in Atlanta on Leeman Bennett's staff, and at one time, we were best friends. He went to work with the Bears in 1980. We stayed in close contact over the next few years. In 1986, I offered him a job as the offensive coordinator of the Oilers. Ted promised me that he would fly to Houston for an interview. Before he came, however, Buddy Ryan went to the Eagles and offered Ted the same job in Philadelphia.

Ted never showed up for the interview. I haven't spoken to him since. And I won't. He didn't have to take the job, but he promised me he was coming for the interview. Everything was set. When you jump out of my boat in the middle of the ride, don't look for a life preserver. In fact, you better hope an oar doesn't hit you in the side of the head.

What hurt me the most after I came to Atlanta was

that I thought Floyd Reese was coming with me. Floyd
had coached linebackers in Houston, and we had worked
together since my college coaching days. I offered him
the job of assistant head coach, and he looked me in the
eyes and accepted with a handshake. The Falcons had
his office cleaned and ready, and even had his nameplate
up over his locker. Then he called me to tell me the
Oilers had offered him the job of assistant general manager if he would stay in Houston. He decided to accept
the job.

I said, "Floyd, you looked in my eyes and shook my
hand and said you'd coach here. To me, that's it, it's
over."

"But Jerry," he said, "I think I've got a chance to be
a GM one day."

"What in hell does an assistant GM do?" I asked him.
"To be an assistant GM, you need a beer gut and have
to know how to play dominoes and smoke a cigar."

I listed every assistant GM I ever knew in my life, and
not one of them was still in football. One is dead, one
is selling insurance, one is in the oil business and
another is an exterminator. Maybe the last guy learned
something from his football job.

But Floyd refused to budge. I told him I'd believe him
when he didn't show up for his first day of work in
Atlanta. He didn't show. I sent him one black rose, with
a card that said, "I'm so sorry to hear about your sudden
death in your profession." I signed it, "A friend from
another life."

Today, Floyd Reese is in charge of signing free agents

for the Houston Oilers. How would you like to go through life with that assignment? I think I'd rather be tied to a tree and whipped.

Floyd won't admit it, but deep down, he's like me. He's a competitor. He lives for the thrill of Sunday mornings. The challenge of beating somebody else. Signing free agents? Please.

When I was an assistant in Buffalo and Floyd was an assistant in Minnesota, I had verbally agreed to go to Houston, but had yet to sign a contract. Floyd, meanwhile, had convinced Mike Lynn to hire me in Minnesota. Before I left for Houston, Floyd arrived at my house with a Minnesota contract. It was for twice as many years and a lot more money than what Houston had offered.

Floyd asked me, "Did you shake their hand?"

I said, "I gave them my word over the phone."

Floyd called Mike Lynn. "We checked with the league; they have no legal right to you whatsoever," Mike said.

I said, "Mike, this may sound crazy, but I told Houston on the phone that I was going, and I'm going to Houston."

Floyd shook his head. "You're a crazy guy, Jerry," he said. "But I respect you for it."

If Doug Shively ever becomes an assistant GM, I'm leaving football. I could never be a GM, or assistant GM. What I love about coaching is crawling out of that dark hole. I don't think anybody was ever in a darker hole than Houston. And now, in Atlanta, we get to crawl out of that sucker again. As we crawl out of that hole, we may have to step on some faces, some hands and some noses, but half the fun is trying to find daylight. Half the fun of the job is trying to find out who you are and what you are and what you'll become.

I've never been to the Super Bowl, but I wouldn't quit coaching if we won it. I can't imagine me doing anything else. If you take a . . . what's the guy's name at Pittsburgh?—that guy didn't quit and he won four Super Bowls. He's still trying to do what he does best. But a general manager? Wear a tie, sit in an office? Nah. Good luck, Floyd.

So here I am, in Atlanta again. And it feels great to be home. They say rebels never stay in one place too long, but I'm going to try to break that trend. I've spent twelve years in Atlanta already, six at Georgia Tech and six with the Falcons. I'd like to stay here forever and get the job done. This may be about as close to heaven as I'll ever get. Won't it be fun to bring great pride back to the city and make everybody in the country know and love our football team? And because of the faith he showed in me, we want to bring Rankin Smith, Sr., a championship football team.

After I was hired, Ken Herock told me something that really caught my attention. He said, "I talked to about one hundred people before I hired you. About fifty loved you. And about fifty hated you. But nobody sat on the fence."

I wouldn't have it any other way. You might hate me, you might love me, but be one or the other. Kris Kristofferson asked me once, "Why do you like listening to old drunks sing?" I said, "I don't know, I don't drink." I've noticed since I quit drinking I haven't been hand-cuffed. Kris tells me that whenever he sings "The Pilgrim" now, he dedicates it to me, because it sums up my whole career.

That's the highest compliment a rebel could have.

See him on the sidewalk in his jacket and his jeans
Wearing yesterday's misfortunes like a smile

Once he had a future full of money, love and dreams,
Which he spent like they were going out of style

He keeps right on a changing
For the better or the worse
Searching for a shrine he's never found

Never knowing if believing is a blessing or a curse
Or if the going up was worth the coming down

He has tasted good and evil
In your bedrooms and your bars
And he's traded in tomorrow for today
Running from his devils and reaching for the stars
And losing all he ever loved along the way.

But if this world keeps right on turning
For the better or the worse
All he ever gets is older and around
From the rocking of the cradle
To the rolling of the hearse
The going up was worth the coming down

He's a poet
He's a prophet
He's a pilgrim and a preacher
And a problem when he's stoned

He's a walking contradiction
Partly truth and partly fiction
Taking every wrong direction
On his lonely way back home

There's a lot of wrong directions
On that lonely way back home

—Kris Kristofferson
"The Pilgrim"

Epilogue

Every football team takes on its own identity and reflects its own personality. I don't know what we'll be in Atlanta, but we *will* have an identity. Everybody from New York to California will have an image of the Falcons. I promise you.

I don't know how our players will respond until we see them in battle. I do know that the players who stay here and play for us will enjoy living on the edge, they will enjoy throwing their bodies on live hand grenades. We will be a team that is known for hunting, chasing and hitting. We will smack you and attack you. In our total package, it doesn't matter what the coaches know, it matters what the players execute best, and that's what we'll do, provided its done in an attacking nature. The Red Gun will be part of us. We'll probably feature different routes because we have different people, and we'll feature different protections because we have different linemen. We'll continue to attack on defense, too.

Another thing—I'm not going to squash anybody's personality. I'm going to let the players' personalities stand out. The first thing I did in Atlanta was meet with Deion Sanders. I was disappointed—he wasn't wearing his Mr. T starter kit. He was without his gold. I tried to explain to him that gold is good luck. The more he wears, the better we'll play. I believe that. I love the kid. I hope my son grows up just like him. He's got personality, he's got identity, and he's got lots of money.

When you think of the 49ers, you think of an identity. When you think of all the good teams of the past, like the old Steelers, the old Raiders, they all had identity. Houston has an identity. We will have an identity in Atlanta. We want men who will stand up and be counted. Men who will make something happen.

We'll keep our old road music, though. Willie Nelson used to help the Falcons in the early '70s whenever we'd go "on the road again" against the 49ers and the Rams, but now I think that Jerry Jeff, John Cougar Mellencamp and Kris Kristofferson ought to be worth a few wins, too. And we'll need them, because when I look at our 1990 schedule, ten of our sixteen games are All-Tylenol games. It's hard to believe, but we play the AFC Central my first year here. Cincinnati and Houston have to play in Atlanta—ain't that special. We play at Cleveland and Pittsburgh. I promise two things this year—that at least twice we'll be booed as good as anybody in the league.

By the time we get done playing the AFC Central and everybody in the NFC West twice, you won't need a barometer to find out how good we are. In the AFC Central, nobody had a losing record. In the NFC West, nobody had a losing record except the Falcons. That will change. Courage will become more important than talent here in Atlanta. It won't matter whether a guy was drafted in the first round or tenth round. Why is every good center as free agent, a guy who's too short and too ugly? Because that's a job where there's not a lot of people applying. It takes courage and toughness. I've never seen a nose tackle with a Ph.D., either.

The last time we were in Atlanta, we had a deal where every time they gave the football to the Bears' Walter Payton, all the Falcons' fans stood up and shook a red towel. After about twenty-eight carries, he had about 24 yards. He wasn't just running against our football team, he was running against Fulton County Stadium.

We'd love to give everybody in the stands a black flag. Then let our players hunt and chase. People forget that the House of Pain in Houston wasn't a building. It was an attitude. When you came down the tunnel, the feeling ran down your body, into your fingers and toes, and set you on fire. That's what we need in Atlanta. We need that tingling, that attitude, that electricity.

The House of Pain will have to be developed in Atlanta through the chemistry of the players, the staff and the fans. Especially fans. When we started in Houston, we had 24,000 fans. When we left, we had 60,000. We were fortunate that we had the right 24,000 to begin with. They came to be part of the spirit. The last game in Atlanta in 1989, there were 7,000 people. But the key is, let it be the right 7,000; people who bring the spirit with them.

There are big challenges ahead. We won't run from anybody on the schedule. I hope what we emphasize will spill over into the city. If the players can feed off the city, then the city can feed off our team. We need them, and they need us.

Somebody told me this team had lots of potential. I believe that the only thing potential means is that the coach is going to get fired. Potential means everybody thinks you have great players and you're not playing well enough. I'd rather have no potential, and results. I'd rather have a bunch of stiffs who play hard, who get after you and leave their guts between the sidelines. Potential means that God gave somebody a lot of ability, but so far he hasn't shown enough guts and courage to go chase and hit. I get nervous and my knees start shaking when somebody starts talking about potential.

It's hard to win the Kentucky Derby riding a donkey. When they swing around that last curve down the stretch, watch and see who goes to the whip and who goes to the hand ride. The thoroughbred always responds to the hand ride. The thoroughbred in football is the star who can win the game by himself and has the guts and courage to do it. We may have to go to the whip early, before our players find out they can win it in a hand ride. And the best jockeys will whip the horse that's trying to pass them, too, right on the nose. That's the way we will be in Atlanta. When the other horses start to pass, they're going to get smacked on the nose.

Now, donkeys *can* win the Derby, but they have to do it in a relay. They just have to hand off the baton about every 10 or 12 yards. But even that requires about ten or twelve good donkeys.

We may have thoroughbreds. We may have donkeys. But we're gonna find a way to win.

And don't be surprised if you see Elvis in Atlanta. I walked in my new office the other day and his sunglasses were sitting right next to a new shiny Falcons helmet. I'm tempted to let him play one more time, just to see how he looks in an Atlanta helmet. We won't throw to him anymore, though, because he's already proven that he can't catch. After he dropped that pass in 1988, we know Elvis don't like football.

But Elvis loves excited, radiant people. Remember this: Elvis lives wherever the spirit is alive.

And the spirit is alive in Atlanta.

—Jerry Glanville
March 1, 1990

Index

Adams, Bud, 131, 138, 141, 159, 161–63
AFC Championship, 135
AFC Central Division, 74, 85, 86, 109, 179, 180
AFL-NFL merger, 133
Agee, Charles, 77–78
Alabama (band), 4
Albert, Marv, 137
Allen, George, 31
Andersen, Morten, 54–55
Anderson, Flipper, 145
Anderson, Gary, 158
Anderson, Loni, 69–70
Arena Football, 113
Arizona, University of, 58
Astrodome, 63, 104, 117, 143, 147, 157
Atlanta Falcons, 8, 28, 36–41, 47, 53, 59, 64, 74, 76, 97–98, 105, 113, 148, 153–55, 159–75, 178–82
Axthelm, Pete, 130–31, 136

Baltimore Colts, 148
Bartkowski, Steve, 40
Bean, Bubba, 76, 77
Beathard, Bobby, 138–39
Belichick, Bill, 33

Bennett, Ben, 113
Bennett, Leeman, 36–37, 40, 41, 172
Berman, Chris, 137–38
Berry, Raymond, 33
Beurlein, Steve, 144
Birdsong, Craig, 77, 81
Birmingham Stallions, 23
Blanda, George, 56
Bostic, Keith, 59
Bouchette, Ed, 95
Bozworth, Brian, 150–51
Bradshaw, Terry, 144
Breech, Jim, 109
Brewer-Georgio, Gail, 6
Brister, Bubby, 86, 142
Brown, Brad, 123
Brown University, 27
Bryant, Domingo, 83
Buck, Ray, 135–36, 139
Buffalo Bills, 16, 41, 72–74, 92, 143, 145, 147, 174
Bugel, Joe, 7, 27–29, 32, 33
Bush, George, 16, 141
Butkus, Dick, 144
Byrd, Richard, 88, 90–91, 109, 149–50

Campbell, Hugh, 41, 44–46
Canadian Football League, 44
Capone, Al, 72

Carley, Jim, 91
Carlson, Cody, 2
Carr, Jimmy, 33, 35
Carson, Bud, 29–31, 33, 40, 114
Chicago Bears, 113–114, 117, 146, 172, 180
Childress, Ray, 109, 150
Christensen, Todd, 63–64
Cincinnati Bengals, 16, 55, 69–70, 108–11, 116, 142, 153, 170, 179
Civil War, 36, 159
Cleveland Browns, 11, 16, 29, 46, 47, 71–72, 80–81, 100, 114, 135, 142, 145, 150, 151, 179
Cleveland Stadium, 71, 81
Cobble, Eric, 77
Coleman, Dabney, 72–73
Conerly, Matt, 78
Cooper, D. B., 70–71
Costas, Bob, 136–37
Coury, Dick, 47
Crawford, Michael, 68

Dallas Cowboys, 41, 71, 103, 111, 113, 115, 155
Dallas Times Herald, 133
Davis, Al, 166
Davis, Bruce, 107
Davis, Mouse, 53–54, 172
Dean, James, 6, 14, 67–68, 164
Defense, 23, 33, 148–56
  in Atlanta, 37–41
  in college football, 26–28
  eleven-man front on, 35
  in Houston, 42–44, 50, 61, 148–53, 155–56
Dennis, Nick, 27
Denver Broncos, 36, 56, 79, 133–35, 142
Detroit Lions, 11, 12, 14, 16, 23, 29, 32–37, 53, 55, 59, 75, 99, 110, 111, 153, 172
Detroit Tigers, 11
Dickerson, Eric, 147
Dierdorf, Dan, 119
Dishman, Cris, 153
Ditka, Mike, 113, 114
Donaldson, Jack, 16
Donaldson, Jeff (Lethal Weapon), 59, 90, 102–3, 153, 155
Dotsch, Rollie, 18, 22–24, 26–27
Dreith, Ben, 115–16, 143
Dukakis, Michael, 141
Duke University, 113

East Carolina State University, 171
Easterling, Ray, 153, 154
Eaton, Tracy, 155–56
Edelstein, Fred, 139
Elway, John, 134, 144–45
Esiason, Boomer, 109, 144
ESPN, 130, 137, 161, 163
Everett, Jim, 145, 147

Federal Bureau of Investigation (FBI), 70–71
Federal Express, 94
Fields, W. C., 68

Florida, University of, 53
Forzano, Rick, 32–38, 40
Fowler, Ed, 128
Fulton County Stadium, 180

Georgia Tech, 29–31, 33, 37, 79, 175
Gibbs, Joe, 115
Gillbride, Kevin, 171
Givens, Ernie, 50, 63
Glanville, Brenda, 31–32, 35–37, 46, 72, 101, 111, 114, 118–19, 126, 161–64, 166, 169
Glanville, Justin, 49, 118, 126, 128, 158–59, 163, 164, 166, 169, 172
Glanville, Richard, 10, 11, 13–15, 17, 20, 136
Glazebrook, Bob, 39–40, 153, 154
"Glowbal" Records, Inc., 4
Gorlitz, Jerry, 22
Graceland, 5, 6, 8
Grant, Will, 147–48
Great Northern League, 16
Green Bay Packers, 23, 35
Greene, Mean Joe, 85, 92
Greenwood, L. C., 92
Greer, Linda, 103
Grimsley, John, 87, 90
Gritz Blitz, 28, 38

Hackett, Paul, 47
Hadl, John, 35
Halas, George, 117
Hand, Kenny, 3, 135–36

Harris, Franco, 146
Harris, Leonard, 83
Hayes, Woody, 151
Helton, Kim, 53
Herock, Ken, 160, 166–68, 175
Herzeg, Ladd, 4, 45–47, 56, 75
Highsmith, Alonzo, 56, 88, 114, 147
Hill, Drew, 50, 90
Holly, Buddy, 71
Holovak, Mike, 45–46, 76–77, 138–39, 159
Houston, University of, 113
Houston Chronicle, 90, 128, 159
Houston Gamblers, 54
Houston Oilers, 37, 41–65, 71, 100–107, 109–11, 113–17, 124, 129, 141, 145, 147, 161–63, 167–70, 172–74, 179
  defense of, 42–44, 50, 61, 148–53, 155–56
  Elvis and, 1–6, 8
  in playoffs, 55, 56, 84, 132–35, 157–59
  press and, 131–36, 138
  rivalry with Pittsburgh, 69, 85–96, 125–26, 157–58
  special teams of, 58–61, 130
  during strike, 74–84
Houston Post, 3, 47, 91
Hudspeth, Tommy, 36

Idaho, University of, 17
Indianapolis Colts, 47, 67
Injuries, 61–62

Interceptions, 38–39, 135
Iverson, Kurt, 133

Jackson, Bo, 146–47, 163
Jackson, Ernest, 87–89
Johnson, Jimmy, 113
Johnson, Kenny, 40, 60, 83, 104, 154–56
Johnson, Walter, 54
Jones, June, 1, 53–54, 75, 155, 171–72

Kansas City Chiefs, 45, 114
Kellermeyer, Doug, 77
Kelly, Jim, 54, 143
Kennedy, Jim, 126–27
Kennedy, John, 21
Kickoffs, 54–55, 58–59
Kidd, Billy, 83
Korean War, 112
Kosar, Bernie, 144
Krauss, Barry, 148
Kristofferson, Kris, 99, 108, 164, 175–77, 179
KSAT-TV, 43

Lackey, Bill (Mojo), 141
Lambert, Jack, 85, 92
Landry, Tom, 60, 111–12
Lang, Gene, 135
Layne, Bobby, 16
Leachman, Lamar, 29
Leyday, Allan, 143
Leyland, Jim, 16–17
Liberty Bowl, 2
Linebackers, 34, 37, 50, 54, 150–52

Lipps, Louis, 86
Lombardi, Vince, 114, 117
London Sun, 4
Los Angeles Raiders, 63, 144, 163
Los Angeles Rams, 37–38, 47, 74, 145, 147, 154, 167, 179
Lyles, Robert, 50, 63, 89, 109
Lynn, Mike, 174

McBride, Larry, 4
McDowell, Bubba, 154
McGuire, Paul, 138
McMahon, Ed, 68
Madden, John, 136, 137
Maguire, Paul, 73
Malone, Mark, 86
Marino, Dan, 143–44
Martin, Charles, 89
Martin, Dave, 14
Matthews, Bruce, 50, 93, 106
Matthews, Clay, 151–52
Meads, Johnny, 50
Mellencamp, John Cougar, 105, 140, 164, 179
Merrow, Jeff, 40, 148
Michigan, University of, 76
Michigan State University, 12
Minnesota Vikings, 23, 29, 47, 152, 174
Miracle, Roger, 16
Monroe, Marilyn, 67
Montana State University, 17
Montgomery, Greg, 105–7

Moore, Sam, 76
Moore, Tom, 29
Munchak, Mike, 49, 50, 93

Namath, Joe, 37–39
Navy, U.S., 29, 32
NBC, 72, 137, 138
NCAA, 30, 32
Nebraska, University of, 47
Nelson, Willie, 97–98, 179
Ness, Elliott, 72
New England Patriots, 1, 2, 4, 23, 36, 57, 82–83
New Mexico State University, 78
New Orleans Saints, 39, 54–55
New York Giants, 45, 115
New York Jets, 4, 16, 68
New York Times, 133
NFL Players Association, 74
NFC Western Division, 179, 180
Noll, Chuck, 8, 19, 21, 51, 69, 85–86, 89–96, 106, 122, 124, 125, 168
Northern Michigan University, 18–24, 26
Nose tackles, 149
Novak, Frank, 22

Oakland Raiders, 79, 95, 166, 179
Offense, 23, 33, 39, 142–48
  in college football, 27
  in Houston, 44, 49, 50, 53–54, 61, 79
Officials, 115–17
Osborne, Tom, 47

Parcells, Bill, 115
Pardee, Jack, 113, 170
Parks, Jeff, 43
Payton, Walter, 146, 147, 180
Pease, Brent, 79–80, 83
Penalties, 51, 135
Pennison, Jay, 50, 88
Perry, Michael Dean, 150
Perry, William (The Refrigerator), 150
Perrysburg (Ohio) High School, 13
Phantom of the Opera, 68
Philadelphia Eagles, 68, 151, 172
Phoenix Cardinals, 7, 27, 137, 172
Pinkett, Allen, 50, 88
Pittsburgh Pirates, 17
Pittsburgh Post-Gazette, 95
Pittsburgh Press, 94
Pittsburgh Steelers, 23, 33, 50, 68–69, 80, 85–96, 106, 118, 122, 124, 125, 142, 155, 157–58, 166, 175, 179
Playoffs, 53, 55, 56, 84, 132–35, 157–59
Plumb, Ted, 98–99, 113, 172
Pollard, Frank, 88, 90–91
Portland State University, 53, 155, 172
Power, Jo Ann, 120, 125
Power, Sam, 120–21
Presley, Elvis, 1–8, 67, 164, 182

Pridemore, Tom, 39, 153, 154
Prothro, Tommy, 36
Punt blocking, 34, 59

Quarterbacks, 40, 50, 56, 134,
    142–44
  hitting, 38
  and interceptions, 39
  replacement, 79–80
  sacking, 42

Rashad, Ahmad, 136
Receivers, 145–46
Recruiting, 30–31
Red Gun offense, 54, 178
Reed, Andre, 145–46
Reese, Floyd, 34, 47, 100–101,
    173–75
Referees, 115–17
Reynolds, Burt, 70
Rice, Jerry, 145–46
Robinson, John, 45
Rogers, George, 39
Ronald McDonald House, 68
Rozelle, Pete, 57
Rozier, Mike, 48, 50, 88, 93,
    134, 147
Running backs, 49, 50, 88–89,
    146–47
Run 'n' shoot offense, 53, 54,
    171, 172
Rutherford, Dr., 19
Ryan, Buddy, 2, 94, 112,
    172

Safeties, 153–56
Salem, Harvey, 52–53

Sanders, Deion, 179
San Diego Chargers, 36, 69,
    138, 139
San Francisco 49ers, 47, 150,
    167, 170–71, 179
Schottenheimer, Marty, 114
Schroeder, Jay, 128, 144
Seale, Eugene (The One-Man
    Gang), 59, 60, 77–79, 83,
    152
Seattle Seahawks, 53, 56, 70,
    114, 133, 149
Secret Service, 16
Senior Bowl, 169
Shephard, Derrick, 59
Sherman, Ray, 170, 171
Sherman, William Tecumseh,
    36
Sherrill, Jackie, 131, 132
Shively, Doug, 5, 37, 47, 53,
    99–100, 103, 104, 154,
    170, 174
Shurmur, Fritz, 33
Silverheels, Jay, 72
Simpson, O. J., 137
Slaughter, Webster, 145
Smith, Al, 89
Smith, Bubba, 75
Smith, Doug, 90, 91, 107
Smith, Rankin, Sr., 161,
    164–68, 175
Smith, Rankin, Jr., 160, 161
Smith, Richard (Perfect), 58–60,
    169, 170
Smith, Taylor, 159, 160,
    163–65
Smith, Tommy, 169

Southwest Memorial Hospital, 121

Special teams, 32–35, 37, 152
  in Houston, 58–61, 130

"Splat" hits, 61, 89

Stagger Lee play, 134–35

Stamps, Sylvester, 146

Staubach, Roger, 32

Steinecker, Bob, 14

Steinkuhler, Dean, 50, 106

Sticky Sam defense, 35, 37

Stoughton, Scott, 77

Studwell, Scott, 152

Super Bowl, 23, 41, 43, 45, 133, 170–71, 175
  XXIII, 111–12
  XXIV, 145

Sylvester, Curt, 136

Tampa Bay Buccaneers, 143, 146

Testaverde, Vinny, 143–44

Texas, University of, at El Paso, 76, 77

Texas A & M, 131, 132

Texas Department of Corrections, 78

Texas State School for the Blind, 77

Theismann, Joe, 3

Three Rivers Stadium, 86, 155

Tight ends, 147–48, 151

Trumpy, Bob, 137

Turner Broadcasting System (TBS), 113

Tyson, Mike, 61

United States Football League (USFL), 23, 54, 75, 171

Utterback, Bill, 95

Walker, Doak, 16

Walker, Herschel, 155

Walker, Jerry Jeff, 105, 108–9, 123, 126, 164, 179

Walsh, Bill, 137

Washington Redskins, 31, 59, 115

Watterson, Steve, 2, 54, 83, 104, 169–70

Webster, Mike, 86

West, Charlie, 153

Western Kentucky University, 27–29

Wheeler, David, 18, 126

Whitacre, John, 14

White, Danny, 41

White, Lorenzo, 102, 157–58

White, Reggie, 150

Wide receivers, 49, 50

Wiley, Ralph, 138

Wilkenhauser, Charles, 69

Williams, Jamie, 55–56, 148, 151

Wilson, Steve, 134

"Window-shade" hits, 61

Woodson, Rod, 158

Wyche, Sam, 8, 55, 109–11, 168

Yeates, Jeff, 148–49

Zampese, Ernie, 145

Zendejas, Tony, 56, 106